HONEST
Conversations

···

Reflections on prayer in the Psalms

DAN THOMPSON

Honest Conversations - *Reflections on prayer in the Psalms*
by Rev. Dan Thompson
© 2014 All rights reserved
www.logoi.org

Editors: Angie Torres-Moure
        Ed Thompson
        Carolyn Thompson
Design: Meredith Bozek

ISBN 978-1-938420-50-4

DEDICATION

This book is dedicated to the church family at
Christ Community Church in Titusville, Florida.
Thank you for giving me the freedom
to spend time week after week in prayer
and in the study of God's Word.

And a special thank you to my wife, Margaret,
who has faithfully prayed with me
and for me for over 30 years.

CONTENTS

Dedication

Introduction 7

    Chapter 1: When You Pray 14

Part I: *"Our Father in heaven…"* 27

    Chapter 2: Is Prayer a One-Way Conversation? 28

    Chapter 3: When God is Silent 40

Part II: *"Hallowed be Your Name."* 53

    Chapter 4: Search Me, O God 54

Chapter 5: THINK Before You Pray 69

    Chapter 6: Talk to God about What He has Done 82

Part III: *"Your kingdom come, your will be done"* 96

    Chapter 7: Thirsty for God 98

Chapter 8: Declare His Glory Among the Nations.............. 110

Part IV: *"Give us today our daily bread..."* 123

Chapter 9: Can You Say Thank You? 124

Part V: *"Forgive us our debts as we forgive our debtors"* 137

Chapter 10: Confession Isn't Enough 138

Chapter 11: A Broken and Contrite Heart.......................... 152

Part VI: *"Lead us not into temptation"* 165

Chapter 12: God Alone 167

INTRODUCTION

It is ironic that I would be writing about prayer! I am not an expert on the subject. I am often disappointed with my prayer life and feel guilty that I don't pray more often or with more passion. I have good intentions but don't follow through. I know some things about prayer, but that doesn't necessarily mean I pray well.

The origin of the chapters that follow is a series of sermons I preached in the spring and early summer of 2013 in response to a request that came from the elders of the church I have served for 24 years. As I was finishing a series of messages on the Gospel of Mark, these men asked me to preach a few sermons on prayer based on the psalms. One man said, "I have begun to realize that I don't know how to pray. I need some encouragement and help to understand the whole subject of prayer."

As I began to prepare messages, my desire was not to give people techniques for praying or a better method for prayer. I've listened to lots of advice through the years about how to pray that hasn't produced a greater desire in my life to actually pray. I know what I should do. It's the desire to do it that is often lacking! So the question I asked was "How do I get my heart to want God more so that I will turn toward him more often and enjoy talking to him in prayer more than I do now? What has to happen in my heart for prayer to be a more natural part of my life rather than a duty I have to perform?"

The reason I liked the idea of talking about prayer in connection with the psalms is that the psalms present a rich portrait of the person and character of God. I don't think anyone is going to pray more or pray better unless their delight in God grows. What better place can you turn to in Scripture to find expressions of delight in God than the psalms?

I began the sermon series with an introduction to the subject of prayer. In our church we have our worship service first and follow that with a time of discussion. I began doing this five or six years ago because I wanted to know what people were actually hearing in the sermons I preached. It's easy for a pastor to assume people understand what he has taught, that the application was clear and people will go home and think about what was said and follow through on the suggestions made for application. But that's not necessarily the case. It's easy for people to walk out after a worship service and say that was a good sermon, and never think about it again! I thought a time of discussion after the sermon might help to reinforce the ideas presented in the sermon each week. So this has been our pattern for several years.

There are always things I'd like to say in a sermon that I have to leave out because of time constraints. The discussion time allows me to take the subject a little deeper. It also gives people the opportunity to ask questions if something wasn't clear in the sermon. And it gives me an opportunity to ask questions that will help people apply the ideas presented in the sermon.

After giving an introduction to the subject of prayer and moving the subject toward the psalms, I invited people to ask questions they have about the subject and practice of prayer. I wrote down their questions and promised to do my best to address some of those questions. Their questions were not a surprise. I've been asked those same questions for years and I've asked many of those questions myself:

"Does prayer really change anything?"

"Why does God often seem so far away? Jesus invites us to ask the Father for what is in our hearts, but what should I think when God doesn't seem to answer my prayers? Sometimes it feels like God isn't even there!"

"Is it right to demand that God listen, like some of the psalmists did?"

"Can we question what God chooses to do in our lives, or is that a lack of faith and an insult to God?"

"What is the relationship between God's sovereignty and our prayers? If God has already determined what he is going to do in a given situation, what difference does my praying make?"

"What role does my faith have in prayers – that is, should I assume the reason God hasn't answered my prayers is that I don't have enough faith, that if I believed more strongly, what I asked would happen?"

"Why should God care about my little requests when he has so many people to take care of in this world? Am I bothering God with my requests?"

As I listened to people's honest questions and wrote them down, it struck me again that what people needed was not a bunch of simplistic answers to those questions. They needed a larger vision of who God is and what it means for us to be in a relationship with him.

Obviously, there is much more that could be said about prayer than I said in these messages. There are many fine books on prayer available for those who would like to read more. There are books available from men and women whose practice of prayer is or was far richer than mine has been, and who would therefore be qualified to give advice that I don't feel qualified to give. Like I said, I am not an expert on prayer – just ask my wife! I need encouragement as much as anyone else when it comes to the practice or praying. So I approach all of this as a fellow-struggler.

What I have tried to do is provide some reflection on the person and character of the God to whom we pray and some application of what the psalms say about God and our relationship to him. I have found that I enjoy prayer more and go to God in prayer more often when I am delighting in the person and work of God.

Most of us probably know some things about prayer. We've heard sermons on prayer and read books or magazine articles about prayer. We know some things about the theory and theology of prayer. It would be easy to convince ourselves that knowing some things about prayer is as good as praying. But knowing some things about prayer is not the same as being a praying person.

As theologian J.I. Packer put it:

"If you get joyfully misty in a library researching prayer, yet end up with no time, energy, or motivation to do more than mumble a few goodnight words to God at the end of the day before sleep sets in, you are not a praying person."

(J.I. Packer in *Praying: Finding Our Way Through Duty to Delight,* p.9)

In an essay entitled, "Meditation in a Toolshed" C.S. Lewis wrote:

"I was standing today in the dark toolshed. The sun was shining outside and through the crack at the top of the door there came a sunbeam. From where I stood that beam of light, with specks of dust floating in it, was the most striking thing in the place. Everything else was almost pitch black. I was seeing the beam, not seeing things by it.

"Then I moved, so that the beam fell on my eyes. Instantly the whole previous picture vanished. I saw no more toolshed, and (above all) no beam. Instead, I saw, framed in the irregular cranny at the top of the door, green leaves moving on the branches of trees outside and beyond that, 90 odd million miles away, the sun. Looking along the beam, and looking at the beam are very different experiences."

Lewis concludes his analogy with an application: "…it is perfectly easy to go on all your life giving explanations of religion, love, morality, honor, and the like, without having been inside any of them… You go on explaining a thing without knowing what it is."

(C.S. Lewis, *God in the Dock*)

The week I came across that essay, I had been in Miami to watch my nephew, David, play his first baseball game as a member of the University of Miami baseball team. I've watched David play baseball whenever I could get to a game from the time he was five or six years old. It has been his dream for years to play for "the U". Because I'm a pastor and had to be home in time to preach on Sunday, I could only watch the first of the three-game series. I listened to the other games on the radio. They won all three games in their opening series and David had a great weekend at the plate!

When he was interviewed on the radio after the series, David said, "Everything I learned about baseball I learned from my dad." That was a really nice thing to say (he loves his dad – my brother, Ed, who has been David's biggest fan all his life). But it was a bit of an exaggeration.

Ed played football in high school and college (or as he puts it, he donated both of his knees to college football). We played a lot of baseball in the backyard while we were growing up. I think all of my brothers and I did a short stint in Little League and played some church league softball when we were in high school. All of us like baseball!

Ed has been watching David play baseball from about the time David could walk. David's first word was "ball." Ed was probably the first one to throw a ball to David so he could hit with a bat. Ed showed him how to throw and catch. He signed him up to play organized baseball as soon as David was old enough. Through the years, Ed has learned a lot about baseball: He has listened to things David's coaches said. He has studied the game. He has watched David play hundreds of games from little league on through high school state championships and now to college baseball. For years Ed and David have gone to baseball games at the University of Miami, they've watched the Miami Marlins live and on television. They even bought the T-shirts when Miami won the World Series in 2003.

By now, Ed knows a *lot* about the game of baseball! He loves baseball. He can talk about it for hours! But aside from backyard and maybe some little league, *he's never actually played baseball!* He has never stood at the plate and faced 90 mph fastballs.

I'm not belittling my younger brother. I'm sure if he hadn't been in a cast after every football season, he probably would have been a good baseball player – he was a good all-around athlete. But as with C.S. Lewis's beam of light, there is all the difference in the world between knowing about baseball and actually experiencing it by playing the game.

I've been a pastor for 31 years. In that time, I have read a lot of books and sermons about prayer by men like Charles Spurgeon, Martin Luther, and others. I've read collections of Puritan prayers. I've listened to some very good sermons about prayer. I have prayed with and for a lot of people – people who were sick, people who were dying, people who came asking for pastoral counseling. I have led corporate prayers week after week, year after year. I have preached about prayer and taught from passages in Scripture that deal with the subject of prayer. But knowing about prayer and actually praying are two different things!

Most of us probably know enough about prayer to convince ourselves that *knowing something about prayer is as good as doing it.* But knowing some things about prayer is not the same as being a praying person.

My desire in going to the psalms to consider patterns and models for prayer is to encourage people to enjoy God and to learn to express that enjoyment by simply talking more often to God. I hope these messages will be an encouragement to you and will stir you up to go to the Father more often and more naturally in prayer.

Chapter 1

When You Pray

*H*ow did you learn to pray?

If you're around Christians for a while, sooner or later you'll hear someone pray like this: "We beseech thee, most gracious Lord and Heavenly Father, to hearken to our petitions as we humble ourselves before you this morning..." For some reason, the person praying thinks God speaks in King James' English!

On the other extreme, I recently heard someone who was asked to pray before a meeting say, "Hey, Jesus! Yeah. We just want to come to you and thank you, Lord..." Hey, Jesus? That's a bit casual for addressing a King, don't you think?

People usually learn to pray by listening to other people pray. You listen to someone you respect as a Christian pray and assume that's the right way to pray. Consciously or unconsciously, you imitate those prayers or at least the vocabulary and style of those prayers.

If you grew up in a Christian family and went to church all your life, the concept of prayer is familiar to you. It's something Christians do or, at least, something they should do. Honestly, the subject of prayer is probably something you feel guilty about. You know you don't do it as well or as often as you should. But at least the idea of praying doesn't sound strange to you.

If you didn't grow up going to church or in a Christian family, the idea of prayer is probably a bit foreign! Imagine you had never visited a church of any kind or heard anything about the Bible. A friend who is a Christian invited you to his home for a Bible study and you thought you'd humor him and go along. It was interesting. A group of people sat around and talked about something they read in the Bible.

Then it got weird! They all closed their eyes and started talking out loud to someone you couldn't see. Nobody peeked. But you did! You thought, "Why are they all closing their eyes if they can't see God anyway?" You listened, and some people in the group talked to God, some didn't. And you certainly didn't because you thought, "I wouldn't know what to say…" You were afraid that if you started talking to God right there in front of other people, even though their eyes were closed, they would recognize your voice and know right away that you didn't have a clue about any of this!

But maybe after a few weeks or months, what you were hearing about God in the Bible made sense, and you became a Christian. You started going to a worship service in a church building. And when you met with a group of Christians, you were finally brave enough to try praying *in public*. You had listened to the other people in the group, and you picked up the vocabulary. So one week, when the group gathered for dinner, you offered to pray before the meal.

Meal time prayers

Your first out loud mealtime prayer probably went something like this: "Heavenly Father, bless this food to the nourishment of our bodies and us to Thy service, in Jesus' name, Amen." And you thought, "I did it! I prayed, and nobody laughed!" You had no idea what those words actually meant, but you prayed in public! Now you knew how to pray. And in time, you even risked saying a bit longer prayer in the group prayer time.

And then you tried it at home. After all, Christians are supposed to pray. So out of a sense of duty, you tried it. You didn't pray out loud, because nobody was around. You just kind of thought the words. And you asked God to help someone who was sick, or to bless a missionary the church supported.

Maybe you tried that for a few days. But after a while, it felt kind of pointless. It wasn't all that meaningful or fun. Honestly, it was kind of boring. You talked to God, but he didn't talk to you! And it was hard to keep your mind focused even for a few minutes. So you decided to leave the praying to the experts (the pastor and worship leaders at church). Once in a while, when something reminds you that you should or when it seems like a good idea, you'll say a short prayer. Other than that, it isn't a part of your daily life.

I suspect *your experience is far more common than you imagine.*

Maybe part of the problem is that we don't understand what prayer is and we've not gone to the right sources to learn how to pray! The psalmist writes, *"Teach me your way, O LORD…"* (Psalm 27:11). He is asking for instruction from God. That's the right source when it comes to learning to pray! If you want to learn how to pray, you need to go to God, through his Word, the Bible. Don't just imitate someone whose praying impresses you. And don't assume you will know how to pray instinctively as time goes by in your life as a Christian.

The right way to approach God in prayer is *learned from God* as he teaches us by his Spirit working through his Word. And he's given us great instruction in Scripture, particularly in the psalms: 150 models of praise, thanksgiving, petition, intercession, and meditation that should inform the way we approach and speak to God.

Teach us to pray

It was unintentional, I'm sure, but the disciples of Jesus echoed the request of Psalm 27 *(Teach me your way, O LORD)* when they asked Jesus *"Lord, teach us to pray, just as John taught his disciples"* (Luke 11:1). Jesus was praying. His disciples saw him and heard him praying. There was something different about the way Jesus prayed. He wasn't trying to impress anyone. It was real and genuine and attractive. He didn't recite memorized prayers, or they could have memorized the words he used and prayed like he did. So they said, *"Lord, teach us to pray."*

In Luke's account, Jesus gave them what we call the Lord's Prayer. In Matthew's account of the same event, he tells us that Jesus first told them some things to avoid.

"Beware of practicing your righteousness before other people in order to be seen by them, for then you will have no reward from your Father who is in heaven…And when you pray, you must not be like the hypocrites. For they love to stand and pray in the synagogues and at the street corners that they may be seen by others. Truly, I say to you, they have received their reward" (Matthew 6:1,5).

Those Jesus identified as hypocrites prayed in order to be seen and admired. They were more concerned about what other people thought about them than they were about what God thought. They weren't praying. They were performing!

When Jesus prayed it was different. Jesus spoke to God like a child speaks to his father. His prayers were spontaneous, full of confidence that God is not distant, but near.

Jesus went on to say, *"But when you pray, go into your room and shut the door and pray to your Father who is in secret. And your Father who sees in secret will reward you"* (Matthew 6:6).

I'm a pastor. I have to pray in public every week! Is Jesus saying it's a bad idea to pray in public? No. It's the heart attitude that matters.

I'm sure you've been in situations where you knew other people expected you to pray out loud. I remember the sheer terror of that when I was younger! The youth pastor asked us to pray around the circle. I was in the circle. Everyone would notice if I didn't pray. I had to say something. While other people were praying, I was counting down how many were left before I had to pray. I practiced what I would say in my mind so I wouldn't sound like an idiot when my turn came around.

Was that prayer? Nope. I wasn't thinking about God or talking to God at all. I was thinking about what others in the group thought about me. I was "praying" to be seen by men, to gain their admiration.

Jesus told his disciples not to be like the hypocrites who make sure they wind up on a street corner at the prescribed daily times for prayer so they can have an audience. They want to be admired. People admire them. They received their "reward" – the approval of other men. But God is not impressed with all that. That's not prayer!

Empty Phrases

Furthermore, Jesus continued, *"And when you pray, do not heap up empty phrases as the Gentiles do, for they think that they will be heard for their many words. Do not be like them, for your Father knows what you need before you ask him"* (Matthew 6:7-8).

Something like what we call "prayer" is happening all over the world right now in all kinds of religions: prayers are being offered to various gods in India, to Allah in the Middle East, to ancestors in some cultures, to saints and to Mary, the mother of Jesus, by Roman Catholics. Christians aren't the only people who pray. But in all this "praying", what can you discern about people's concept of God or their gods by the way they pray?

Maybe you've seen pictures of prayer wheels in the mountains of Nepal. To a pinwheel, driven by the wind, scraps of paper with written prayers are attached. Just think how often that prayer comes around on a really windy day! What do those who attach their prayers to a "prayer wheel" think the gods are like? What seems to matter is not the heart of the person praying, but the number of times the prayer goes out! The gods are moved to respond by the number of times a request is made. The person making the request isn't sure what that number is (how many times the prayer needs to go out to get the attention of the gods) but they get the petition going around over and over again, hoping they'll hit the right number and get a response from the gods.

In Islam, devout Muslims pray to Allah at prescribed times, five times every day. No matter where they are when the call to prayer comes, they kneel, facing the right direction, bow before God, which is the correct posture, and repeat prescribed prayers. You've probably seen pictures of Muslims on their knees touching their foreheads to the ground on their prayer mats. Day after day they follow this prescribed pattern for prayer as part of their devotion to God.

There's probably something we can learn from the Buddhists about being persistent in praying for something that is important to us. And there's something we could learn from the Muslims about being devoted to consistent prayer. But what kind of God is impressed more with the sheer volume of words and hours spent praying than with the heart attitudes of the person praying? What kind of God would care more about the time of day when you pray than about the desires and attitudes of your heart?

Jesus told us not to be like the Gentiles who think they will be heard because they use a lot of words. On the other hand, what does the way you pray and the words you use when you pray reveal about what you believe God is like? Where do meaningless words creep into your prayers?

A little help, please

Jack Miller, the founder of World Harvest Mission, said he once asked his wife, Rose Marie: "If you could change one thing about me, what would it be?" She said, "You don't listen." So Jack began to pray, "Lord, forgive me for not listening to my wife. Help me to be a better listener."

Do you see any problem with that prayer? From just those words, what did Jack Miller believe about God and about himself? By saying, "Help me," Jack was saying, "God, I can do it. I can be a better listener with a little boost from you. All I need is a little help!"

A year later, after asking God to help him be a better listener, he came back to his wife and asked, "Rose Marie, if you could change one thing about me, what would it be?" And she said, "You don't listen." He was shocked. He said it took him a while to understand that he couldn't change himself with just a little help from God. He needed a changed heart. And only God could change his heart. That began to change the way he prayed. Instead of just saying, "Help me do this," he began to ask God to change in him what he could not change through his own efforts. Sometimes when we ask God for help, we recognize our dependence on him. But sometimes it can be "empty phrases" – words that sound pious but don't mean anything.

Where else do we tend to repeat prayers that become empty words? What about our prayers before meals? How often have you heard or prayed something like this: "Bless this food to the nourishment of our bodies..." That sounds pretty spiritual! So you've picked that up and used those words. But what does that mean?" Would the food not be a blessing or nourish your physical body if you didn't ask God to use it like that? Is it like God performs a special miracle when you ask him to bless the food to the nourishment of our bodies? Does he remove the germs that would have made us sick if we hadn't prayed? Is that the reason for praying before we eat?"

What do you mean when you ask God to "bless this food"? I was at a family gathering one time and one of my nephews came in late for dinner. Everyone greeted him, and someone said, "Sit down and eat, the food has already been blessed." What does that mean? Does it mean we recited the prescribed magical incantation to invoke the protection of the deity over the food? It's now safe to eat!

Isn't the reason for praying before a meal to remember that everything comes from God? Jesus taught us to pray, *"Give us today our daily bread."* God has given us food to eat, so we come before him and remember our dependence on him and express our gratitude for his blessing of food and drink.

Instead of a bunch of meaningless words repeated time after time, Jesus told his disciples to pray sincerely. It's the heart that matters, and what you believe God is like will shape the way you pray!

Prayer has to do with relationship

If you talked to your wife only when other people could see and hear what you said, and if your motive was to impress them with what a wonderful husband you are by the lovely things you say, do you think your wife would want to hear you talk? She wants you to talk to her, not with flowery words you've memorized or by saying exactly the same things you've said every day for years. She wants you to really talk to her! She wants you to want to know her and to let her know you by telling her what you think and how you feel about things that have happened.

God is a person. He has spoken to us in creation and more clearly in his written Word. He has given us his Spirit to open our minds to what he says in his Word. And he invites us to talk to him, to express what we're thinking, what we're feeling, what we're afraid of, what we don't like, what we do like.

A pattern for prayer

Having warned them against praying just to impress others and against repeating meaningless words, Jesus gave his disciples a pattern for prayer. We call it the Lord's Prayer, but it is not something Jesus prayed over and over again. It can't be! It includes the petition, *"Forgive us our debts* (our trespasses).*"* Jesus never needed to ask the Father to forgive him. He never sinned! And having just warned his disciples not to make prayer a matter of repeating words over and over again, he certainly would not have given them a prayer they should memorize and pray word for word day after day. There's nothing wrong with reciting the Lord's Prayer in a worship setting. But it is a pattern for prayer that Jesus gave us.

He said, *"Pray then like this: Our Father in heaven, hallowed be your name. Your kingdom come, your will be done on earth as it is in heaven. Give us this day our daily bread, and forgive us our debts, as we also have forgiven our debtors. And lead us not into temptation, but deliver us from evil"* (Matthew 6:9-13).

In the chapters that follow we are going to be looking at patterns for prayer that can be found in the psalms. What you find in this model prayer Jesus gave us are aspects of prayer that are deeply rooted in the psalms. The Lord's Prayer is a model prayer, a pattern for praying. Jesus gave his disciples some categories of things to pray about. And you will find all of those categories of prayer in the psalms. In a sense, the skeleton of the Lord's Prayer is fleshed out in the psalms.

Let me explain by briefly showing how each of the petitions of the Lord's Prayer can be found in the psalms.

Our Father in heaven

No devout Jew before the time of Jesus addressed God as "Father". Jesus introduced that close relational term. The psalmists, writing hundreds of years before the time of Jesus, did not address God as "Father". That is a distinctively Christian way to address God. But as you consider the various ways the psalmists addressed God, what you find are terms that imply an intimacy of relationship.

"O LORD, our Lord, how majestic is your name in all the earth" (Psalm 8:1)!

"O LORD, my God, in you do I take refuge" (Psalm 7:1).

The term LORD (all caps) in our Bible translations is the word *Yahweh*. When Moses met God at the burning bush and God commanded him to go back to Egypt to tell Pharaoh to set the people of Israel free, Moses said to God, *"If I come to the people of Israel and say to them, `The God of your fathers has sent me to you,' and they ask me, 'What is his name?' what shall I say to them?' God said to Moses, 'I AM WHO I AM.' And he said, 'Say this to the people of Israel, I AM has sent me to you'"* (Exodus 3:13-14).

When a psalm begins by addressing God as LORD, it is this revealed name of God that is used. It can be translated literally as "I Am," but in the Old Testament covenantal context, it means "I am with you to bless you."

So the name of God as the psalms begin reflects an intimacy, closeness, and a certain privilege that belongs to the people of God. Jesus intensified that sense of intimacy with God by encouraging us to address God as "Father," but biblical prayer has always assumed a relationship of closeness with God.

Hallowed be your name

Prayer is concerned with God's glory. The psalms are a rich source of not just information about God, but of learning ways to delight in the majesty and beauty and glory of God. God is holy. God is high and exalted. He is transcendent – high above us. Our Father in heaven is infinitely holy, and that creates a certain amount of reverence and awe as we come before God. We are sinful people – forgiven, justified, adopted, but still sinful. Even so, we are invited to draw near to God as loved children!

This petition, *"hallowed be your name"* has its parallel in the psalms: *"Exalt the LORD,"* *"Magnify the LORD!"* To exalt is to lift up from a lowly position to a position of honor. To raise in status, dignity and honor. We can't make God any higher status than he already is! We can't make God more dignified or more worthy of honor. We can't make God more holy than he already is. So why do the psalmists call us to exalt and magnify God? What higher status can you lift him up to? What higher position can be given to God than King of kings and Lord of lords? Who is higher than the Most High God?

To exalt God means to elevate or lift God higher in our estimation of him. In the way you think of God, may he be hallowed and honored with the respect that belongs to him.

Your kingdom come

God rules over all. He is sovereign over men and nations. In this petition we are not asking God to begin to reign. We are expressing a longing for the visible reign of God to spread in this world. We are asking that people, including ourselves, would honor God and acknowledge his lordship.

If God is reigning as the Sovereign King over all the earth, why is there so much evil and brokenness in our world? The psalms will give you examples of the kind of honest questions you can bring to God and the perspective God will give you as you ask those questions! The psalms are full of expressions of desire for God's reign to be evident in life. The longing expressed in the psalms is for the peoples and nations of this world to know and honor God.

Your will be done on earth as it is in heaven

Prayers in the psalms are often focused on the difficulties people experience in this fallen world. What we experience in life doesn't make sense if God is ruling over everything. What goes on in our world often doesn't look like the will of a good and loving God. We are often confused – what we experience doesn't fit the ideas we have of how God should work in our lives! So God's people cry out to him for justice, for change, for understanding.

Give us this day our daily bread

Because we can go to the grocery store and buy what we need without any difficulty, and because we have food in the pantry and the refrigerator, it is easy for us to forget that God is the one who provides what we need to live each day. When you are out of work and can't find a job and bills begin to pile up, you are forced to recognize how desperately you need God to provide what you need to live. When you are hungry and a meal is provided for you, being thankful is easy. When you have all you need, it's easy to forget to thank God for his provision!

The psalms are full of thanksgiving and gratitude for God's provision for his people. The writers of the psalms expressed dependence on God for everything.

And forgive us our debts, as we also have forgiven our debtors

We are sinners. Sin creates a relational debt to God – we haven't honored him as we should. We sin against God, we sin against other people, and other people sin against us. Jesus taught his followers to acknowledge their debt of sin before God regularly, to face the truth about what our sin does to our relationship with God, and to know that we need God's forgiveness. Sometimes we understand how our sin impacts God by feeling the impact of other people's sins against us!

There are great examples of remorse, confession and repentance in the psalms. We need to learn that there is a difference between merely admitting that we have sinned and actually turning to God in repentance and acknowledging our need for God's mercy and grace. The psalms give us a deeper understanding of what it means to pray, *"forgive us our debts..."*

And lead us not into temptation, but deliver us from evil

It won't take you long as you read through the psalms to find the psalmists asking God for protection, acknowledging their weakness and looking to God to rescue them from their enemies, from opposition, and from evil. There is honesty in the psalms about the brokenness of our world, about the evil we suffer and about the sense we have when we suffer wrong that we need a defender and an avenger.

The temptation when we are sinned against is to take vengeance into our own hands. We don't just want to get even; we want to get ahead in the score! But we end up making things worse!

Furthermore, experiences of being wronged often lead to temptation to reject God. The lies and temptations of Satan haven't changed through the centuries: "Did God really say that? God knows that won't happen. God is not good, he is holding something back from you that would be good for you." In those times when God allows us to experience suffering or to be sinned against in a grievous way, we will experience temptation to not believe God is wise in what he chooses and that he is not good in what he does.

The psalms teach us to bring those ways we've been wronged to God and plead with him to deal with those who have sinned against us – to *deliver us from evil.* And the psalms bring us back from our unanswered questions about God's work in our lives to remind us that God is good and wise in all he does.

Prayer is a privilege

The psalms were not written to give us a method for praying or to provide instruction on the right technique for prayer. They are actually a collection of songs. But in those songs of praise and adoration and confession and petition, we can learn much about the God to whom we pray.

I'm not saying we need to go beyond what Jesus taught us about prayer. I'm saying what Jesus said is also found in the psalms. Jesus knew these songs and prayers of Israel. They were on his mind often – even as he hung on the cross (Psalm 22 begins and ends with words Jesus cried out on the cross). The God Jesus described when he taught his disciples to understand God's willingness to hear their prayer is the same God you find in the psalms.

Biblical prayer assumes this truth about God: He is a person who wants to know us and wants to be known. A force or an impersonal power can't hear or respond. God is a person who hears, who cares, who invites, who loves, who protects, and who delights in being known.

The privilege of approaching God like this is staggering! Jesus is uniquely the Son of God, and God is uniquely his Father. When Jesus prayed, He came to his Father as the one and only Son. But now he makes it clear that those in relationship with him have been brought into this intimate relationship with God. We can now call God "Father" and come to him as loved children.

Ultimately, it's what we believe about God in our hearts that will shape the way we pray.

PART I

"Our Father in heaven…"

*J*ESUS TAUGHT US TO PRAY TO GOD AS "FATHER." One key aspect of the Holy Spirit's work in our lives is to convince us that we are adopted sons and daughters of God. He teaches us to cry out to God as "Abba! Father!"

If God is our Father, why does it often feel like prayer is a one-way conversation? It often feels like God is far away, hard to reach, unconcerned with our daily lives. Often we ask God to intervene in a difficult situation or to show his glory and power by changing circumstances that need to change, but God doesn't seem to intervene and the circumstances don't change. Why does it often feel like God doesn't listen when we pray?

The psalmists remind us in many ways that God is not silent – he is speaking every day in ways that are clear and personal. And the psalms invite us to pour out our hearts to God when life doesn't make sense and it feels like God is far off.

Chapter 2

Is Prayer a One-Way Conversation?

T WAS AN AWKWARDLY SILENT WAY TO BEGIN a seminar on prayer. Before he began to teach, Paul Miller asked those people who had come to learn more about prayer to spend five minutes praying. Then he asked them to tell him what they experienced in those five minutes of silence as they prayed. People responded:

"It felt like a one way conversation. I did all the talking."

"It was boring."

"Time seemed to drag by – it felt more like 10 minutes. I found myself wondering, 'isn't five minutes over yet?'"

"My mind wandered. I couldn't stay focused."

"It's like God isn't there and I'm just thinking words."

After he had written their responses on a white board, he read them to the group and flipped back to what people had said in previous seminars. Then he asked what they would think of someone who described their relationship to their earthly father like this:

"When I talk to my dad, it's like a one way conversation. He never says anything! It's boring. My mind wanders. I can't stay focused. Time seems to drag by."

What would you think of that person's relationship with his father? Talk about a dysfunctional relationship! That is a pretty sad relationship! What kind of cruel father would sit there and say nothing while his son tries to carry on a conversation? What kind of son has a hard time enjoying even five minutes talking to his dad?

The point Paul Miller was making is powerful: The way we pray says a lot about what we think God is like as our Father. The battle to enjoy prayer is not learning right techniques. Rather, it is about discovering who our Heavenly Father is and understanding how he speaks to us.

At the dawn of creation, Adam and Eve walked with God in the garden and talked with him face to face, like friends who take a walk together in the afternoon. But when Adam and Eve rebelled against God, they were put out of the garden and a fierce angel with a flashing sword guarded the way back to the garden. The message was clear: they had lost face-to-face access to God. Their sin now kept them from the immediate presence of God.

The amazing promise of Scripture is that the day is coming when we will see God face to face. We will be with God and enjoy the kind of face-to-face conversation with God that Adam and Eve enjoyed in the garden. But what about now? Jesus said we ought always to pray and not give up. He warned us not to use prayer as a tool to impress other people with how spiritually mature we are, or to let it become a kind of meaningless babbling, repeating words that have lost any real meaning for us. He gave us a pattern for prayer. So obviously, Jesus, our Savior and King, wants us to pray!

Prayer is not just for some people. It's for all of us who have been saved by God's grace! God wants us to pray. But what has your experience been with prayer? Many of us would say: "Honestly, it feels like a one-way conversation. I do all the talking and God is silent!"

Prayer confusion

What makes it all the more confusing is that you have Christian friends or have heard Christians say: "I was praying the other day and God said to me…" You thought to yourself: "Really? God spoke to her? Why doesn't he speak to me?"

On the other hand, when you've heard people talk about what they claim God told them, it makes you wonder if they were hearing God or imagining things. Sometimes the things people claim God told them are pretty harmless. Sometimes the words they claim came from God sound like something from the Bible (and it is intriguing that God still speaks King James English!). But sometimes it gets more than a little strange!

A man once told me God had assured him he would marry a single woman in the church. As things unfolded, it seems God neglected to inform the woman! And when the man told her God had said she should marry him, she had her doubts! She married someone else. And this man was convinced she had chosen to go against God's will!

I heard another man teaching about how to hear from God. He said all the thoughts going through your mind all the time are God's way of speaking to you! And if you'll just slow down and listen to those thoughts, you'll hear from God. I thought, "Do I really want to attribute to God many of the thoughts that go through my head? I don't think so!"

When it comes to the subject of prayer and listening to GOD as part of prayer, there are a lot of confusing ideas. I don't want to defend or deny what people claim about how God speaks to them – God is free to do far more than I can imagine. But the Bible is clear that God *is communicating with us all the time!* And if you're going to grow in terms of enjoying prayer and delighting in God, you have to believe that God is communicating, and you need to hear what he is saying!

The reason for prayer

The reason the Bible invites us to pray and encourages prayer is because, when God visits his grace on us, we are brought into a relationship with God that is *not* like a slave/king relationship. A king doesn't want to know what the slave is thinking or feeling. He doesn't care what his slave thinks or feels. He just wants the slave to be quiet and work hard.

That's not what our relationship to God is like!

"But when the fullness of time had come, God sent forth his Son, born of a woman, born under the law, to redeem those who were under the law, so that we might receive adoption as sons. And because you are sons, God has sent the Spirit of his Son into our hearts, crying, 'Abba! Father!' So you are no longer a slave, but a son, and if a son, then an heir through God" (Galatians 4:4-7).

If God has saved you by his grace, if God has given you life by his Spirit, something inside you begins to turn instinctively toward God as Father. "Abba" is a term of intimacy, like when my daughter calls me "Daddy." One of the powerful ways the Holy Spirit works in God's people is to convince them that God is their Father:

"For you did not receive the spirit of slavery to fall back into fear, but you have received the Spirit of adoption as sons, by whom we cry, 'Abba! Father!' The Spirit himself bears witness with our spirit that we are children of God, and if children, then heirs – heirs of God and fellow heirs with Christ…" (Romans 8:15-17a).

When you think of intimacy in marriage, one of the simplest ways to define intimacy is as the experience of being close to another person. Intimacy is knowing someone and being known in a safe and secure environment. It is enjoying someone and having that person enjoy you. Intimacy grows out of giving yourself to another person and having that person give him or herself to you.

God created us with the capacity to know and be known and with a need to know and be known. And it is the process of communication that fulfills this need. Communication is essential to a marriage relationship. In many ways, you don't know yourself until you have to express what you are feeling and thinking to your spouse. As you express your deepest thoughts and feelings, you begin to understand yourself better.

Communication, in marriage or in a good friendship, requires sharing not only facts and ideas, but talking about what you are feeling – disappointment, fear, grief, joy, hopes, longings.

That has not been easy for me in marriage. I have been afraid that if I told Margaret what I thought or how I felt about something, she wouldn't like me. What I've found is that we've actually grown closer as I have learned to share my heart. And I have grown to understand what is driving my heart as I've tried to express my thoughts and feelings. I know her far better than I did when we were first married, and she knows me better. We understand more clearly how different we are in temperament, how differently we respond to the same situation, and we know now how to love and encourage each other far better than we did at the beginning of our marriage. That growth has come through a long, sometimes difficult struggle to communicate with each other.

The same is true about prayer. As you listen to what God is saying about himself and about you, and as you tell God what is in your heart – doubts, questions, things you can't understand, things that make you angry, things you like or dislike – your intimacy with God will grow deeper, your love for him will grow stronger, and your confidence in his goodness and faithfulness will become more unshakeable!

Constant communication

The psalms tell us that God is communicating with us all the time. When I tell you how God is doing this communication, you're going to say, "Oh, yeah. I knew that…" But I remind you that knowing something in your head is one thing. Believing it in your heart and experiencing it in practice is something very different. You can know a lot about something without ever having experienced it for yourself. This is what the Scriptures affirm about God speaking to us:

God speaks to us every day through the things he has made.

God speaks to us more clearly through his written Word.

You know that theologically. But what does this have to do with prayer? I want you to consider the fact that prayer is not a one-way conversation with you doing all the talking and God remaining silent. To the degree you believe this, it will inform and shape the way you approach prayer and the enjoyment you find in prayer!

A language everyone understands

In one of our hymns we sing, "In the rustling grass I hear him pass, he speaks to me everywhere." Have you ever thought about what you were saying when you sang those words and thought, *"Really? God speaks to me everywhere?"* Yes, the psalmists affirm. God speaks every day, loudly and clearly!

> *"The heavens declare the glory of God; the skies above proclaim his handiwork. Day to day pours out speech, and night to night reveals knowledge. There is no speech, nor are there words, whose voice is not heard"* (Psalm 19:1-3).

To declare something means to announce clearly – to speak out! To proclaim means about the same thing: to state, to declare. Hebrew poets found beauty in parallel statements, not in rhyming lines. To *pour out speech* means there is a steady flow of words. What God is saying through his handiwork is clear in every language in the world! God is a master communicator!

But it's one thing for someone to speak – even to speak well and clearly. It's something different for people to understand what is being said. If someone came into our church service, ran to the front of the auditorium and started declaring something important and proclaiming it loudly in Japanese, none of us would understand a single word that was said.

God's daily proclamation is not in a language we can't understand!

"There is no speech, nor are there words, whose voice is not heard" (Psalm 19:3). No matter what language or what words someone uses, what God is saying is clear. It gets through. His words go out (v. 4) *"to the end of the world."*

By declaring the truth about himself and proclaiming things about himself through what he has made, the message is communicated to people in every culture, in every language, in the entire world, in a language they can understand. There are truths about God that he is literally shouting from the skies every day of our lives!

I live in Florida. Sometimes in the spring, the smell of orange blossoms is inescapable. I love the time of year when Azaleas bloom in all their rich colors. We don't
get much of a seasonal change in Florida, but there is something sweet about the first
cold front of the fall, when the humidity drops and there is finally the hint of coming
change. Season follows season in predictable order. Birds that have been gone all
summer begin to show up again and we hear their songs in the woods behind our
house. Soon the oranges will be ripe and we'll get to taste their sweet flavors again!

Step outside a cold, cloudless night and look at the stars. If we climb out on the
roof of our house that faces the back yard, the main arch of the roof blocks out the
light from the streetlight out front. Sometimes we climb out there to gaze at the stars.
My whole family was out there one evening to watch a meteorite shower that was
spectacular.

Focus on the full moon with good binoculars or look at pictures of distant galaxies from the Hubble telescope on the Internet. They are indescribably beautiful!
Depending on where you live, you experience tornados, earthquakes, powerful thun-
derstorms or even hurricanes. You see the power of nature in those terrifying and
destructive forces.

God is constantly talking to us

What is God saying about himself through these things we see and smell and
taste and feel and hear? He is constantly telling us, "I am majestically glorious! I am
frighteningly powerful. I delight in a rich variety of color, sound, taste, smell." He is
saying, "I am good! I am the God who provides for birds and fish and animals daily.
I am beautiful. I am greater than you imagine! There is order and design in the universe because I am a God of order and intentionality."

There is an amazing variety of plant and animal species in our world. Scientists
tell us hundreds, even thousands of species are now extinct that were once common
on this planet. Think of the person with the creativity to invent such variety and the
power to actually make what he thinks up! What is God saying? He is declaring, "I am
infinite in wisdom."

In Romans 1, the apostle Paul says nobody will be able to stand before God on the Day of Judgment and say, "I didn't know you existed!"

"For what can be known about God is plain to them, because God has shown it to them. For his invisible attributes, namely, his eternal power and divine nature have been clearly perceived, ever since the creation of the world, in the things that have been made…" (Romans 1:19-20).

You say, "Yeah, I can't believe so many people don't believe in God creating the universe but choose to believe in a mindless, unguided natural process of evolution as the explanation for the origin of the universe! I believe what the Bible says about creation." That's great! But do you *value what God is still saying* to you day after day through what he has made?

Does seeing and tasting and smelling what God has made move you to say: *"I will remember the deeds of the LORD; yes, I will remember your wonders of old. I will ponder all your work, and meditate on your mighty deeds.…What god is like our God? You are the God who works wonders…"* (Psalm 77:11-13).

The psalmist is probably talking about remembering the great things God did in Israel's history as he made himself known to his people. God delivered them from their enemies. He fed them. He led them in the wilderness. But I think the psalmist is saying more than that when he says, *"I will ponder all your work."*

God is communicating constantly! If anyone could think prayer is a one way conversation most of the time, it would be God. He speaks constantly. He declares his glory and power and majesty everywhere, every day. And once in a while we respond!

Delighting in what God has made is part of prayer in the psalms. *"When I consider your heavens, the moon and stars which you have put in place"* (Psalm 8:3).

Think of it this way: if your dad was a world-renowned artist, and you were on a visit to his house and he showed you his latest painting, would you say, "That's nice, but let's talk about something more important. I need your help with…" It's fine to ask your father for help, but wouldn't it be nice to be interested in what he has expressed through his art? Wouldn't it be honoring to him to look carefully at the way he has poured his heart into his art?

If you want to know an artist, looking at what is important to him through something he has made will tell you things about what he loves! The first time you look at his painting, you might say, "That is very nice...I really like that!" The more you look at it, the more you are able to tell him specifically what you like about it or what you don't understand.

We need to learn to see God and to hear God's voice in what he has made and to enjoy and delight in God in prayer by responding to what he is saying! It is prayer to say to God, "I like that. How kind of you to let me see that. How glorious you must be to have made something this beautiful! If this world is fallen and still so glorious, what is the future world like that you are preparing for us? I long for that world... and I long for you!"

How else does God speak to us?

"The Law of the LORD is perfect, reviving the soul;

"The testimony of the LORD is sure, making wise the simple.

"The precepts of the LORD are right, rejoicing the heart.

"The commandment of the LORD is pure, enlightening the eyes;

"The fear of the LORD is clean, enduring forever.

"The rules of the LORD are true, and righteous altogether.

"More to be desired are they than gold, even much fine gold. Sweeter also than honey and drippings of the honeycomb. Moreover, by them is your servant warned; in keeping them there is great reward" (Psalm 19:7-11).

"Blessed are you, O LORD; teach me your statutes.

"Open my eyes, that I may behold wondrous things out of your law.... I will meditate on your precepts and fix my eyes on your ways. I will delight in your statutes; I will not forget your word....O how I love your law! It is my meditation all the day.

"How sweet are your words to my taste, sweeter than honey to my mouth.... I am your servant; give me understanding, that I may know your

testimonies" (Psalm 119:12,18,97,103,125).

The affirmation of Scripture is that God is communicating clearly all the time through his works and through his Word. We sing:

"He speaks and listening to his voice new life the dead receive,

The mournful broken hearts rejoice, the humble poor believe....

Hear him, ye deaf; his praise, ye dumb, your loosened tongues employ."

Learning to hear God

The question now is, "How do you learn to hear God as he speaks through his Word?" The simplest answer is found in Psalm 1: *"In his law the righteous man meditates day and night."*

Listen as Scripture is read publicly in worship. Read it for yourself. And then think about it. Meditate on it.

That word scares some people. Meditation techniques usually try to help people empty their minds as a way of relieving stress and anxiety. That's not what the Bible means by meditate. When the psalmist says, *"Oh how I love your law! It is my meditation all the day"* (Psalm 119:97), it clearly means he is thinking about what God has said throughout the day.

Take a little time to get some portion of God's Word before your mind and you have something to mull over and think about. As you do that, understand what you have read in the Bible is not just what Moses or David or Paul said. This is what God says.

*"All Scripture is **God-breathed...**"* (2 Timothy 3:16).

*"Long ago, at many times and in many ways, **God spoke** to our fathers by the prophets..."* (Hebrews 1:1).

This kind of mulling over what God has said creates a kind of dialogue in your head. You can tell God what you like about something you've read or what you don't understand and ask him to give you insight.

Furthermore, as you ponder those words, God's Spirit personalizes it. You begin to hear God saying to you: *I have removed your sins as far as east is from west. I have loved you with an everlasting love. I have adopted you as my child! I want you to know me as your Father.*

God is speaking to you by his Spirit through his Word. Now you respond to him! You can say, "Father, I believe what you have said, but help my unbelief! You satisfy my thirst, but I keep drinking from other fountains. Forgive me. Change my heart." As I say this, you are probably thinking, "Okay, but what you're describing is still not like someone sitting down and talking with me face to face. It still feels like prayer will be a one-way conversation."

What you feel is not the ultimate determination of what is true! I am encouraging you to believe what the Bible says – that God is daily, tenderly communicating his power, his reality, his faithfulness, his goodness, his sufficiency, and his love for you. These are not just figures of speech.

God wants us to really know him

This is the truth! God wants intimacy with you. He made you to know and be known. And he wants you to know him and experience his presence and power. He is not far off somewhere and therefore hard to contact. He is near. He is *with* you. He is *in* you through the gift of the Holy Spirit.

It is God's Spirit who opens our minds and hearts to believe what God says. God is the one who gives us ears to hear and hearts to believe what God has said in his Word. God's Spirit is the one who leads us to apply God's Word personally, so the message doesn't just stay a kind of generic letter to the human race, but becomes a letter from God to you about his love for you!

It might help to start with reading some of God's Word. There is great value in Bible reading plans. Most of those plans have you read through the psalms once or twice in a year.

As you read some portion of Scripture, ask yourself, "What does this passage tell me about God? How does this point me to Jesus? What does it say about God's love for me?"

Let that passage and its applications roll around in your mind and let it sink into your heart. Tell God what you like about it. Tell him what you don't understand – he won't be offended if you're confused about something or if you don't understand something. Ask him to open your eyes to see wonderful things in his Word.

Thank him for the things he has promised you. Praise him for things you are seeing about his character.

God invites us into this relationship

God walked and talked with Adam and Eve in the Garden of Eden when the world was new. Someday God will walk with us and talk with us. Then it will be face to face, like it was in the Garden when the earth was young. But will you believe that being God's child by his grace means God welcomes you to this kind of relationship now? The Bible doesn't promise that someday God will be with you. It promises that he is always with you! He will not leave you alone. He will never leave or forsake those who have been rescued by his grace. And God invites us to enjoy this relationship as we delight our souls in him in worship and prayer.

Chapter 3

When God is Silent

AS I WRITE THIS, it was almost two years ago that I got the phone call telling me my dad was being taken into emergency surgery. I drove down to Miami and was able to see him in the recovery room and he seemed to be doing well. He was moved to a private room in the hospital, but a couple of days later, he had to be taken back into surgery. Knowing the first surgery had failed, Dad was sure he was about to die. My mom and my brother were the only ones with him and the doctor encouraged us to gather the family since it didn't look like Dad would live much longer.

As our family began to arrive and step in to visit with him, Dad got stronger. He rallied. He prayed with his grandkids and was able to tell them what they meant to him. For a while it seemed that he would recover. But good days would be followed by bad days. He was in the hospital and then a nursing home for about two more months before he died. In those two months, he was in pain, he wanted to die, he pleaded with God to let him die to end the suffering, and God didn't let him die.

I felt so helpless. I wanted him to live, but not like he was. I listened to his prayers asking God to take him, and I started to get angry with God. I asked God, "Why will you not grant his request and let him die? He's ready. He's in pain. Why will you not end his suffering?"

There was a time when a man came to Jesus and said, "...*if you can do anything, have compassion on us and help us. And Jesus said to him, "If I can! All things are possible for the one who believes. Immediately the father of the child cried out and said, "I believe; help my unbelief"* (Mark 9:22-24). The man didn't say, "If you are willing" but "if you can." "Can" implies ability. He was saying, "Jesus, if you are able to do something, I'd appreciate it." In his reply, Jesus brings out this man's doubt about his ability and power to heal.

The reason I felt angry about God not answering my dad's prayer is that I believed God could do what my dad was asking. God is able to heal. If that's not what he was going to do, God was certainly capable of letting my dad's misery end by allowing him to slip peacefully from this life into God's presence. It felt cruel. God let him suffer day after day, for weeks!

If I believed that God wanted to answer his prayer but was powerless to act, I would have no reason to be angry! But what I believed about God actually made it harder to accept his silence!

In the grand scheme of things, what my dad experienced is inconsequential compared to what other people experience. His suffering did come to an end and he slipped into God's presence peacefully in the end. But there are many people I know who have experienced the silence of God; people who have prayed and asked God to do something and it never happened.

There is an elderly lady in our church family who has been bed-ridden for six years. She never married, so she has no children to visit and care for her. For several years, every time I visited her she would whisper to me, "If I sign a letter and give my permission, could you have a doctor give me a shot of something that would let me go to sleep and not wake up?" For six years I've watched her grow weaker and weaker. She has wanted to be able to die, but her body won't let go. She has pleaded with God to let her die, but he has not given her what she asked for. She is going to die sooner or later. What would be so bad about letting her go?

I have another friend who has asked God for many years to let her find someone to marry. She doesn't want to live her entire life single and lonely. But God hasn't answered her prayer.

I have a friend who lost his job a couple of years ago and has been unable to find another job. He has asked God to allow him to have any job, but no job opening has come to him. Our church family has joined him in asking God to provide a job, but so far, he doesn't have a job.

A godly woman in our church family is the only Christian in her extended family. One of her deepest desires is that some in her family would come to faith in Christ. She has prayed for years for the conversion of family members, and no one has come to Christ.

I have a close friend who has prayed for years that God would bring change to his marriage; that his wife would show some sign of really wanting to be married to him. But it hasn't happened.

I have friends who have pleaded with God to give them freedom from a sinful habit that has enslaved them, but they can't seem to find that freedom.

I have another friend who was diagnosed with cancer. She prayed for healing, and God healed her body as she went through chemotherapy. But I have another friend who was diagnosed with cancer, prayed for healing, suffered through chemo and radiation treatments, and died.

I think of a couple in our church family who would be great parents and who prayed that God would allow them to have children. But they have never been able to conceive a child.

World Religions

If you were a Hindu and believed in Karma, you would feel sad about things like cancer, job loss, inability to have children, and death of loved ones. But you would not think something was wrong or get angry about it. It's just karma, and nobody can change karma. The Sanskrit word "karma" means "actions" or "deeds." Specifically, karma is a way of understanding what happens in life when things are difficult. The actions and deeds in view are those done in a previous life that affect what someone experiences in this life. The law of karma says all life is governed by a strict system of cause and effect, action and reaction. What happens to anyone in this world is the direct result of things done in a previous life. It is a way of explaining evil and misfortune in the world, especially when bad things happen to someone who doesn't seem to deserve it. It must be that they did wrong things in a previous life. And if that's the case, they have no one to be mad at but themselves!

Muslims who experience suffering or disappointment in life feel sadness like anyone else. But they don't think something is wrong. They've been taught to believe that fate can't be changed. All people can do when they suffer is to submit to God's will and accept it. They have to resign themselves to the way things are. It won't help to be mad at God. God is not going to change his will to suit a human being!

Christian Assumptions

But as Christians, as people who read and believe the Bible, there are a set of assumptions we bring to prayer: God governs this world. He is Almighty. He is able to do what he chooses to do. Nothing can stop God from doing what he wants to do. There is no power higher than God, like fate, that God has to submit to. And he is good, kind, generous, and giving, a Father who is more loving than any human father. God is not far away and unconcerned about what happens in our lives. He is near us. And he invites us to bring our concerns to him and to ask for things that matter to us.

Where did we get the idea that God is like that? From God himself: *"As a father shows compassion to his children, so the LORD shows compassion to those who fear him..."* (Psalm 103:13). We get the idea that God is good, compassionate, caring, and eager to hear our requests from Jesus, who is God in flesh: *"What father among you, if his son asks for a fish, will instead of a fish give him a serpent; or if he asks for an egg, will give him a scorpion? If you then, who are evil, know how to give good gifts to your children, how much more will the heavenly Father give the Holy Spirit to those who ask him!"* (Luke 11:11-13). The parallel passage in Matthew 7 puts it like this: *"how much* *more will your Father who is in heaven give **good things** to those who ask him!"* God is not like the unjust judge in Jesus' parable who gives in because he's tired of hearing someone complain. It is not hard to get his attention, like the prophets of Baal on Mt. Carmel who spent half a day calling out, *"O Baal, hear us!"* while they cut themselves to show how sincere they were. God isn't like that! He is aware of our needs before we ask him!

The apostle Paul tells us to think of God as one who is *"able to do far more abundantly that all we ask or think..."* (Ephesians 3:20). And Jesus added to our expectations for prayer when he said, *"Ask, and it will be given to you; seek, and you will find; knock, and it will be opened to you. For everyone who asks receives, and the one who seeks finds, and to the one who knocks it will be opened..."* (Matthew 7:7-8).

As Christians we are not fatalists who just have to submit to whatever happens as the unchangeable will of God. We don't believe in karma that is unchangeable or that our suffering is somehow deserved by our own behavior in past lives. We know we live in a fallen world. We experience the brokenness of our world just like people who don't have faith in Christ. We suffer, we get sick, we lose our jobs, and we die, because we share in the fallenness of the human race.

A time of tension

But we also believe God is redeeming us from this brokenness. He saved us in hope (Romans 8) that the world will be set free from its bondage to decay, and that we who are the adopted sons and daughters of God will be set free from all the ways sin affects our world and our lives. But we live in the time of tension, the time between the coming of Jesus and the final restoration of all things when God wipes away every tear from our eyes. And we groan inwardly, Paul says in Romans 8, while we wait for the redemption of our bodies.

Sometimes that groaning is because we don't understand why God chooses to work in our lives in some particular way that makes no sense to us. It's because we believe in a personal, caring, loving Heavenly Father that our times of groaning are intensified. We know God could change our circumstances – he's not bound by fate or karma. We believe he governs in wisdom and that he is good. So we go to God in prayer and cry out, "Why are you so far away from answering my prayers? Can't you hear my groaning?"

But what happens? In our experience, we often ask and don't receive. And we don't understand why that would be! James says in his letter, *"You ask but don't receive because you ask with selfish motives."* Certainly that's true at times. But not always! Our experience is that we ask, believing God is able to intervene and change a difficult situation, but it feels like God isn't there. Nothing changes. God doesn't respond. We ask, but don't receive. Our experience clashes with God's revelation in Scripture and we end up wondering, "If God is good, why is he letting this happen?"

In her book, *Walking Away From Faith*, Ruth Tucker writes:

"...Mom's death was something I could not easily reconcile with my perception of God. The accident was not a twenty-car pileup in a northern Wisconsin blizzard. It happened on a clear afternoon in early autumn at a remote intersection of a country road. And to add insult to injury (and to death), it occurred a stone's throw from my mother's childhood home...and three miles away from the farm on which I grew up. I had crossed that intersection (which had no stop sign) hundreds of times, and never had there been an approaching car. But on this day there were two cars approaching the same intersection, and neither driver saw the other one in time to stop.

"Already struggling with abstract doubts, I now had very personal doubts about the God I worshiped and how this incident, this accident, fit into my faith. 'All things work together for good' – I know the verse (Romans 8:28) by heart. But no, no, no! I screamed, all things don't work together for good. And in this case, if there truly is a God out there who is all powerful, why, O God, why, I asked, did you not prevent this terrible accident..." (p. 21).

That is a question that only makes sense if you believe God could prevent a terrible accident. If you believe God is all-powerful and also good, some of the things you experience in life will not make sense. And if you pray when you face a difficult or painful or life-threatening situation, believing God is able to change your circumstances, but things don't change, your beliefs will be tested: have you misunderstood the promises in the Bible about prayer? Have you misunderstood the character of God?

Let's be honest

We are not alone when we ask these questions. You find the same kinds of questions being asked in the psalms:

"Why, O LORD, do you stand afar off? Why do you hide yourself in times of trouble?" (Psalm 10:1)

"How long, O LORD? Will you forget me forever? How long will you hide your face from me? How long must I take counsel in my soul and have sorrow in my heart all the day? How long shall my enemy be exalted over me? Consider and answer me, O LORD my God; light up my eyes, lest I sleep the sleep of death, lest my enemy say, "I have prevailed over him," lest my foes rejoice because I am forsaken" (Psalm 13:1-4).

"My God, My God, why have you forsaken me? Why are you so far from saving me, from the words of my groaning? O my God, I cry by day, but you do not answer, and by night, but I find no rest..." (Psalm 22:1-2).

"Give ear to my prayer, O God, and hide not yourself from my plea for mercy! Attend to me, and answer me. I am restless in my complaint and I moan, because of the noise of the enemy, because of the oppression of the wicked. For they drop trouble on me, and in anger they bear a grudge against me. My heart is in anguish within me; the terrors of death have fallen upon me..." (Psalm 55:1-4).

Asking these kinds of questions make some people very uncomfortable. It's one thing to read these in the psalms, but to verbalize similar questions can be disturbing for Christians. For some reason we think Christians shouldn't talk like this! You know from experience that sharing these kinds of thoughts and feelings with Christian friends tend to produce unhelpful, trite sounding advice: "Well, you know, all things work together for good…" "You just need to have more faith!" "Maybe you have some sin in your life that is keeping God from hearing you." Job's friends are alive and well in the Christian community!

But let's be honest. What happens in your heart when you plead with God for something that really matters to you? How do you respond when you are confident God is able to do far more than you are asking but it seems God remains silent? What happens when what you ask of God doesn't happen or when God seems far away? How have you experienced the silence of God? Have you experienced God feeling distant? And what are we to do with that experience?

As a pastor, I've talked to a lot of people who have given up on the whole idea of prayer because they have experienced God as distant and silent. People tell me, "Prayer doesn't work." When I ask what they expected to happen, I hear their grief, their disillusionment, their anger at God because of the disappointment they've experienced with prayer. They say, "God didn't come through for me." "It felt like nobody was there. I prayed but God never responded."

Learning from the psalms

The first thing we can learn from psalms (like the ones above) is that it is okay to ask God these kinds of questions. It's okay to give voice to what you're feeling. God isn't offended if you ask why he seems so far away, so silent. These psalms are part of Scripture, inspired by God. The psalms teach us how to praise God, how to delight in God, how to thank God, how to confess our sins and come to God in repentance.

And given the number of psalms that contain laments and questions about God's silence, I suggest the psalms also teach us how to pray when what God does in our lives doesn't make sense. Part of prayer is telling God about the tension we experience when what we believe to be true about God doesn't seem to fit what we experience in life.

These psalms don't offer us techniques for getting God to do what we want him to do. They do not suggest you need to wake him up, point out where he's failing, so that he'll hop to it and do what you think should be done. Part of our problem with prayer is that our expectations are shaped by our own definitions. Jesus tells us to ask. He tells us our Father in heaven is not distant or uncaring and that he will respond quickly to his children who cry out to him! So we think God answering our prayer means granting what we request by doing exactly what we ask of him.

The psalms teach us that it is good and fitting to pour out our confusion to God in prayer. Like the psalmists, you can tell God what doesn't make sense and ask him to give you perspective. You need to know why you can trust God and believe what he says in Scripture even when your experience of God's providence is confusing. As you read these psalms of lament, these cries for understanding, many of these psalms resolve into expressions of confidence in God. Even though they don't receive and answer to all their questions, the psalmists still express trust in the character of God: he is wise and good, he is full of steadfast love for his people.

It may be that in time, you will come to understand why God did not do what you asked of him. His silence at some point in your life may make sense as time goes by. But it also may be that you will not know in this life why God chose to work in your life the way he did. Can you still trust him? Can you rest in his love? Can you rejoice in his goodness?

Ultimately, the questions you have to ask are these: who is going to decide what is best for your life – you or God? What criteria will you use for deciding what is true about God – your experience or God's revelation of himself in Scripture?

It helps me to find expressions of confusion about God's providence in the psalms. It helps me to know I am not alone in the experience of crying out to God and feeling like he is distant and silent. And it helps me to see those expressing these feelings to God still clinging to God in faith. There is something about being honest with God, about telling him what we are feeling and pleading with him for under-standing that helps us regain perspective.

Our feeble sense

"God Moves In Mysterious Ways" is a hymn written in 1774 by William Cowper. I hear people use that phrase as a figure of speech to say "We'll never be able to make sense out of what God does." They shrug their shoulders and resign themselves to the fact that what God does is mystifying. But that's not what Cowper meant. He was expressing confidence in God! When you go through a tragedy or a difficult experience of some kind, the words of the hymn give this counsel: "Judge not the Lord by feeble sense but trust him for his grace."

"Feeble sense" describes our senses that are limited and weak. We know so little of what God is doing! Yet we make judgments about God based on our limited understanding: "He's not acting like a good God." "He isn't doing what is wise or best in this situation." But those conclusions come from our small understanding, our limited, feeble sense of reality.

Instead, Cowper urges us to trust God for his grace! Our confidence, he says, is this: "Behind a frowning providence He hides a smiling face." A "frowning providence" means those times when it seems like God is mad at you or like he has removed his smile or approval because you don't feel like he is blessing you. In those times, what you need to know is that God's smile has not been removed from you. It's hidden for you behind the "frowning providence." But God's smile of approval for you as his adopted child has not changed. His love for you has not changed. You may not see it, but he is always acting in love toward you.

Cowper didn't look at life through a pair of rose-colored glasses. He knew the reality of suffering and evil. But he did deny the idea that evil and suffering are the final word – that they win in the end. It takes gospel courage to hold on to God in the face of "a frowning providence."

Here are the words of his hymn:

God moves in a mysterious way His wonders to perform; He plants His footsteps in the sea, and rides upon the storm.

Deep in unfathomable mines of never-failing skill, He treasures up His bright designs, and works His sovereign will.

Ye fearful saints, fresh courage take, the clouds ye so much dread, are big with mercy, and shall break in blessings on your head.

Judge not the Lord by feeble sense, but trust Him for His grace; Behind a frowning providence, He hides a smiling face.

His purposes will ripen fast, unfolding every hour; The bud may have a bitter taste, but sweet will be the flower.

Blind unbelief is sure to err, and scan his work in vain; God is His own interpreter, and He will make it plain.

Can you trust him?

What if God doesn't make it plain in your lifetime? What if you never in this life come to an understanding of why God chose to allow whatever it was or why God didn't choose to do what you thought would be good? Can you trust him?

The value of voicing your complaints, your confusion, your anger or frustration over what feels like God being distant and silent is that it helps to put things in perspective! It deepens your understanding of God!

*"How long, O LORD? Will you forget me forever? How long will you hide your face from me? How long must I take counsel in my soul and have sorrow in my heart all the day? How long shall my enemy be exalted over me? Consider and answer me, O LORD my God; light up my eyes, lest I sleep the sleep of death, lest my enemy say, 'I have prevailed over him,' lest my foes rejoice because I am forsaken. **But I have trusted in your steadfast love; my heart shall rejoice in your salvation. I will sing to the LORD, because he has dealt bountifully with me***" (Psalm 13:1-6).

You may not understand what God is up to in your life, but this is what you can know about God: He is good, compassionate, kind, patient, long-suffering, abounding in steadfast love. He is wise – he knows what is best in every situation. He is competent – omni-competent. There is nothing that happens in our world that God is not able to handle!

We focus on how the world impacts us. God is governing a world with billions of lives that intersect and impact each other. And he is weaving all these stories together perfectly, to accomplish the greatest glory in the end.

God has an inviting heart. He is not offended when we tell him what's in our hearts. He invites us to come and ask, and he promises to give us the Holy Spirit to comfort and counsel and guide us.

Few people consider that maybe their disillusionment is the result of mistaken views of God, or mistaken assumptions about life! Maybe the problem isn't God, but what you expect God should be and what you expect life should be.

When you are young, people ask you, "What do you want to be when you grow up?" In your mind, you begin to write a script for your life: "I'm going to go to college, get a good education, find a good job, get married, have a few children, enjoy life, eventually retire and enjoy the fruit of my life's work." But life rarely follows the scripts we write for ourselves. We do the same thing in terms of life as a Christian: "If I do these things right, God will bless me. And being blessed by God looks like this…" We have a mental script for how life should go as a follower of Jesus. But God rarely follows our scripts. When you feel discouraged or disappointed, ask yourself, "What did I want? What did I expect was supposed to happen?" That's where you'll begin to see your expectations (your script).

Somewhere along the line we need to realize that God is writing us into his story, not coming alongside to help us write our own stories. He pulls us into the grand story of redemption that he is writing. And his plans and purposes for us are far greater than the plans and purposes we have for ourselves.

The grace to trust him

There's another old hymn that says, "Oh what peace we often forfeit, O what needless pain we bear, all because we do not carry everything to God in prayer." It's very likely, if you grew up singing that hymn, that you took those words to mean if you just prayed about things, peace wouldn't be disrupted and pain wouldn't come into your life. But what happens when you pray and peace is shattered? What do you think when you pray, but pain doesn't go away? There is no promise in the Bible that assures us we will never experience pain or loss of peace if we just pray enough!

What the hymn writer says is helpful if you understand what he means: You aren't big enough to carry the pains life sends your way, but God is! Take those pains to him. Ask him to give you the grace to trust him when he doesn't do what you thought would be best. Ask him to give you the ability to trust him. You don't have to bear "needless pain" if you will learn to take everything to God in prayer. You may not understand what God is up to, but you can know why God is worthy of your trust. And as you tell him what is confusing and hard to bear, God will renew perspective. You are not alone. God isn't silent. He is not distant. He has put his Spirit inside you. It is God's Spirit who leads you to cry out, "Abba, Father," and assures you that God's smile or approval has not been removed.

Judge not the Lord by feeble sense,
But trust Him for His grace;
Behind a frowning providence
He hides a smiling face.

— William Cowper

PART II

"...Hallowed be Your Name."

WHY IS GOD'S NAME NOT HONORED IN THE WORLD AS IT SHOULD BE? If God created and sustains all that exists, why do people not recognize, respect and honor God? For that matter, why do I not honor God in my heart and mind as He deserves to be honored?

When Jesus taught us to pray, *"hallowed be your name,"* he taught us to be concerned with God's reputation in the world. We are to ask God to work in our lives in such a way that we could consider him holy.

The psalms encourage us to ponder the glory and majesty of God. Spending time pondering what God has said in his word, and pondering God's works in creation, providence and in redemption help us develop a larger view of who God is. A desire to honor him as he deserves grows from a larger grasp of the greatness of God.

Chapter 4

Search Me, O God

Y WIFE AND I RECENTLY WENT TO THE APPLE STORE in the Florida Mall in Orlando. I didn't know people still went to malls. I was wrong. It was crowded. There are more than seven billion people in the world right now. About a third of them were in the Apple store the night we were there! There were people from Brazil, China, Central America, and at least two people from Florida. I don't like crowds. My wife loves crowds. I love my wife, so I was willing to be with her in a crowd.

The biggest crowds I've ever been in were in football stadiums. My dad was an avid Miami Dolphin football fan back in the late 1970's, when the Dolphins were a winning team. He had season tickets at the old Orange Bowl in Miami that had seating for 72,000 people. I remember going to games with my dad and feeling like a sardine in a can! I remember looking at all those people and thinking, "I don't know any of these people and they don't know me!"

I live in what a lot of people would consider a small town – just under 44,000 people. It's amazing how rarely I see people I know even in a town this size. When I go to Walmart, I see people I have never met. I can feel lost in the crowd even in Titusville, Florida!

There are millions of people who claim to be Christians in the world right now. On a typical Sunday in the state of Florida, there will be somewhere between two and three million people in church.

Have you ever wondered, "How can God know all these people? How can God care about one person –me– when there are so many people in the world?"

A friend in our church family once said, "There are so many people with real problems. I don't want to bother God with my little problems." He couldn't imagine God being able to handle the prayers and needs of so many people.

On a Sunday morning, when all those people are in churches all over the world, how can God listen to each person's prayers when they are all praying at the same time? How can God keep up with all those prayers?

You know the theological answer: God is omniscient. He knows all there is to know. He is infinite in knowledge.

One amidst billions

But when you feel like just a number in a huge crowd; when you feel insignificant in relation to a big world, it's hard to believe that God really knows you or that he actually wants to know you!

"It is good to give thanks to the Lord, to sing praises to your name, O Most High" (Psalm 92:1).

You can be thankful and express thanks to a large institution that doesn't know your name. I am thankful to the University of Miami for letting me enroll as a student and for the education they gave me. I am thankful that they let me graduate!! Sometime when I'm feeling thankful, I could write a letter of thanks. If I'm feeling particularly thankful, I could send a donation to the alumni fund.

Having driven on highways in foreign countries, I am thankful for good highways in the state of Florida. I could write a letter of thanks to the highway department.

I am thankful for safety and peace in America. I suppose I could write some letters of thanks to the military services or to the FBI.

But I am one person out of millions! I would probably be a rarity if I took the time to say thanks, but still, I would be thanking institutions that don't know me and don't particularly care if I'm thankful or not!

The person who opens my letter of thanks might see my name and appreciate my kind words. But they would soon forget about me and I would still be an unknown individual in a big crowd, speaking to busy administrators and bureaucrats who have a lot to do. There's no personal relationship involved in an expression of thanks to an institution.

Prayer can feel like that. The psalmists tell us *"It is good to give thanks to God."* Good for whom? Good for me? Certainly it is: it makes me humble to acknowledge that where I am in life is due to the kindness of a God who has provided for me in all kinds of ways. It makes me less selfish and self-centered to stop and say thank you. It's good to stop and remember specifically how he has been good to me.

But I am one person in a world with billions! Does God really know me? Or when I pray is it like the angelic scribes are writing down notes to keep track, because God is pretty busy with more important details?

"Rejoice in the Lord; again I will say, Rejoice. Let your reasonableness be known to everyone. The Lord is at hand; do not be anxious about anything, but in everything by prayer and supplication with thanksgiving, let your requests be made known to God" (Philippians 4:4-6).

To say *"The Lord is at hand..."* means God is near. He is not far off in heaven, unaware of your concerns. It's not like he doesn't know what's going on in your life unless you somehow get his attention. He is near.

We know that is true theologically. We believe that in our heads. But we don't believe that in our hearts. We don't live like God is at hand. We don't act like he's close to us.

How does God know us?

How do we get a sense of God's nearness to us into our hearts? How can we pray with a sense that God hears us, that God cares about us, that God has time to listen to us even when millions of people are praying to him at the same time?

Psalm 139 is a meditation: the psalmist is reflecting on the truth that God knows us intimately. As he thinks about God's personal knowledge and speaks about this before God, he provides a great model for us. We would do well to ponder the things he says in this psalm and to pray the prayer at the end of this psalm.

Let's walk through it.

"O LORD, you have searched me and known me!

"You know when I sit down and when I rise up; you discern my thoughts from afar. You search out my path and my lying down and are acquainted with all my ways" (Psalm 139:1-3).

"Search," "know" and "discern" are cognitive words. God analyzes me, examines me, tests me, and knows what is true about me. When he says God is acquainted with all *"my ways"* he's not talking about God knowing where he had traveled that day as he walked the streets of his hometown. He's talking about his character and conduct.

He says, *"God, you know me as I am spiritually. You know who I am at the core."* For God to know like that doesn't mean he has gathered all the data and recorded it in a heavenly computer that he can access later. The word know in the Bible is a word that often implies intimacy *"Now Adam knew Eve, his wife, and she conceived…"* (Genesis 4:1).

For God to know someone like this implies a choice and intimacy, it implies care and protection. It might feel a bit threatening to think that God knows you completely. But God's knowledge is not adversarial – he is not gathering information on you to use against you on the day of judgment. His knowledge is loving! It is personal. It is intimate. This is the staggering truth: God wants to know you. He actually chooses to know you!

Notice the contrasts in the first half of the psalm: sit down, rise up; on the path – lie down; behind – before; go, flee; the heavens – *sheol* (the grave); darkness – light/day. There is no situation you can imagine where God would be unaware of what's happening to you. God is all knowing and everywhere present! God knows you.

Sometimes that is a comforting thought, sometimes that is a very frightening thought! I'm not sure I want anyone to know me like that!

Psalm 139:4 *"Even before a word is on my tongue, behold, O LORD, you know it altogether."*

Is that a comforting thought? Probably not. God knows what you're thinking! In one way, it is amazingly comforting to hear that God knows me completely. But that kind of knowledge is also uncomfortable. And that discomfort is there in the words and imagery the psalmist uses:

Verse 5: *"You hem me in, behind and before, and lay your hand upon me."*

Bruce Waltke says these are actually military metaphors! To hem me in has a chilling tone. The metaphor implies hostility. It can be translated, *"to lock up"*. The second half of verse five continues with this threatening imagery: You *"lay your hand upon me."* Waltke writes: "When one rests his hand on another, the object is decisively under the subject's control, not his own." God's hand can shelter you. But "more often the figure signifies the imposition of a will opposed in some way to another's own" (Bruce Waltke, *The Psalms in Christian Worship*, p. 549).

Verse 6: *"Such knowledge is too wonderful for me; it is high; I cannot attain it."*

That God knows me like that stirs up respect and awe. It also stirs up fear! Such knowledge is *"too high"* for me. This is another military term. The word can be translated, "impregnable, secure." He's saying, "I don't have the power to get above your knowledge. I am powerless before you."

Do you really want God to know you like that?

"God's knowledge is being imaged as a cliff that even a warrior of David's caliber is no match for" (Waltke). All he can do is bow under the mystery and power of God's knowledge. The truth of God's infinite knowledge leaves you feeling amazed, overwhelmed, and a bit restless inside.

Verse 7: *"Where shall I go from your Spirit?"*

He's talking about God's Spirit. As pure spirit, God is not limited to being in one place at one time. So you can't find a place to get away from God!

"...Or where shall I flee from your presence?"

Most of the time when the word translated "flee" is used in Scripture, it means running from grave danger! That's some amazing honesty! God knows what I'm thinking, what I long for, what I have said, and what I have done. God's presence can be comforting at times, at other times it feels downright dangerous! He is infinitely holy and I'm not holy. It feels confrontational for God to know me like that. Being in God's presence makes me feel overwhelmed by my sinfulness. And there is no place to go to escape God. There is nowhere to hide from his searching eye.

Verse 8: *"If I ascend to heaven, you are there! If I make my bed in Sheol, you are there!"*

The contrast means the highest and the lowest places in the universe. Heaven would be the preferable space to be, the place of God's presence. The grave, Sheol, is the place of the dead. You would think you could escape God's frightening presence when you're dead. But no, he is actively present in the realm of the dead.

We can't go up high enough or down deep enough to get away from God. What about east and west?

Verses 9-10: *"If I take the wings of the morning and dwell in the uttermost parts of the sea, even there your hand shall lead me, and your right hand shall hold me."*

Morning breaks in the east, so to *take the wings of the morning* is a way of describing the sunrise. The *uttermost parts of the sea*, for people who lived in Israel, meant looking toward the west. So east or west, as far as you might go, God is there. The sun set over the Mediterranean Sea. If you keep going west, in this imagery, you end up in darkness.

Verses 11-12: *"If I say, 'Surely the darkness shall cover me, and the light about me be night,' even the darkness is not dark to you; the night is bright as the day, for darkness is as light with you."*

Bruce Waltke says, "Darkness in the Bible is more than the absence of light: there is something about the darkness that is destructive to life! It is a realm that is cut off from light, hostile to that which provides safety, freedom, and success; it is the realm of evil and of the wicked…of disaster…and of death…" (*ibid*, p. 556).

But even those dark places are not dark for God!

Lovingly, carefully, uniquely created

Psalm 139 is probably best known in Christian circles for these next verses:

Verse 12: *"For you formed my inward parts; you knitted me together in my mother's womb."*

Think of a weaver, skillfully weaving threads together to make a beautiful tapestry. God created us like that. He created each of us with that kind of personal care and artistry!

We know about DNA and genetics: when your mother's egg and your father's sperm came together, 23 chromosomes from each parent were combined in a unique sequence, unlike that of any other person who has ever been born. All the information that told those cells how to divide and which traits to bring out in you were there from the moment of conception.

You won't hear scientists who understand and study genetics and the DNA code praising the creator of the DNA strand very often. Sadly, for many modern scientists, God has no place in their view of reality. But scientifically, that's how God made you! He used the genetic information passed down from your parents to shape you.

But the psalmist is not making a scientific statement about genetics. He knew nothing about the genetic code. He is making a theological statement: God's thoughts were directed toward you in your mother's womb. God did not passively observe the developing embryo in your mother's womb – he actively programmed it. He wrote the code and sovereignly brought together the genetic information that produced you! As one who had grown up in an agrarian society (David had been a shepherd, after all), the psalmist knew something about hereditary characteristics that cause the offspring to be like the parent. But he looks behind that and sees God at work in the formation of each individual human being.

Verses 14-16: *"I praise you, for I am fearfully and wonderfully made. Wonderful are your works; my soul knows it very well. My frame was not hidden from you, when I was being made in secret, intricately woven in the depths of the earth. Your eyes saw my unformed substance; in your book were written, every one of them, the days that were formed for me, when as yet there were none of them."*

God is writing a story, and he has written you *into* his story! He made you the way you are for his good purposes. Loving care is implied in God's work of fashioning you in the womb. God chose when and where you would be born. He determined ahead of time how many days you would live even before you were one day old.

He knows everything about you. He knows far more about you than you know about yourself! You don't understand why you have certain genetic characteristics, but God does. You don't know how many days you will live on this earth, but God does.

Verses 17-18: *"How precious to me are your thoughts, O God! How vast is the sum of them! If I could count them, they are more than the sand. I awake, and I am still with you."*

So far, so good. But why are these next sentences in this psalm?

Verse 19: *"Oh that you would slay the wicked, O God! O men of blood, depart from me!"*

Caring how God is treated

It may be that pondering God's intimate care and love makes him think of how God is treated in our world. He is ignored, hated, dismissed, and considered irrelevant. If you love someone, it hurts you to see that person mistreated or maligned.

Still, to ask God to slay the wicked is unusual, even in the psalms. Usually the petitions you find are pleas for deliverance from those who hate God, maybe asking God to deal justly with them, to punish them for their evil. Here, he asks God to destroy them.

Verse 20: *"They speak against you with malicious intent; your enemies take your name in vain!"*

He has been speaking honestly and respectfully about God. But there are a lot of people who speak hatefully and disrespectfully about God.

Verses 21-22: *"Do I not hate those who hate you, O LORD? And do I not loathe those who rise up against you? I hate them with complete hatred; I count them my enemies."*

I'll let Bruce Waltke explain this kind of language: "He hates those who hate God, not with malevolence and vindictiveness, but because in the covenant community God's enemies are Israel's enemies. **In this spiritual battle there can be no middle position"** (Walkte, p. 565). *"I hate them"* doesn't just mean I don't like them. Zeal for God comes through powerfully in these words. "His zeal for God could not be stated more emphatically than within these dozen words; unrestrained zeal is necessary to counter effectively the enemy in the battle of religious affections" (Waltke, p. 566).

John Calvin put it like this: "Our attachment to godliness must be inwardly defective if it does not generate an abhorrence of sin, such as David speaks here of" (quoted by Waltke, p. 567).

David has been speaking honestly, in contrast to the false, hateful language of those who hate God. But he also knows that his motives may not be pure. So he shifts gears and asks God to assess the truth of his words:

Verses 23-24: *"Search me, O God, and know my heart! Try me and know my thoughts! And see if there be any grievous way in me, and lead me in the way everlasting."*

Instead of resisting God's knowledge of his heart, he lays his heart open and bare to God. He feels like his motives in asking God to destroy the wicked are clean, but knows that he doesn't know his own motives.

Know my heart

So he pleads with God, *"Search me. Test me."* He doesn't ask God to search and test his enemies. He says, *"Search me."* He is asking God to do an examination of his heart that only God can do. And the purpose of this search is that God might know him intimately and completely, in the depths of his being – *"know my heart."* In biblical imagery, your heart is the place of your deepest thoughts, motives, desires, longings and feelings.

Having asked God to destroy the wicked, it's as if David thinks, "Am I as completely devoted to you as I just said I was? I need God to show me if there is any wicked way in me." "If" means the psalmist doesn't know with certainty what's there in his heart.

The prophet, Jeremiah, said: *"The heart is deceitful above all things and desperately wicked, who can know it?"* (Jeremiah 17:9). He doesn't say, "Once my heart was deceitful and wicked, but now that I have come to love God, my heart is pure. It no longer deceives me. It no longer produces sin." He says the heart is still is beyond his ability to cure it!

David is saying something similar. He is unable to know and judge his own heart completely. There are depths to it he can't fathom. There are motives there that he doesn't understand, desires he doesn't see.

Only God knows what it is in your heart!

For God to find an "offensive way" in your heart means for God to see some offense that causes God pain. As frightening as it might be for God to search you like this and to show you what's in your heart, it is by opening yourself to God like this that you change!

"His own integrity is not sufficient for this. His own ways could, in fact, carry him toward pain and destruction. Only if Yahweh will lay his hand on him, to guide, sustain, and control him utterly, can the poet hope that his ways will conform to Yahweh's way" (Lovitt, quoted by Waltke, p. 569).

Uncomfortable Intimacy

You and I *say* we want to learn to pray and to experience more joy in prayer. We say we want a deeper intimacy with God. But the truth is, there is a part of each of us that doesn't want that!

Intimacy can be defined as the experience of closeness that comes from knowing and being known in a relationship that is secure. It's fine to know more about God, but it is uncomfortable to think that God knows more about me than I want him to know – more than I know. It's frightening to think that He knows what's in my heart!

By nature, as sinners, we do what Adam and Eve did in the garden – we hide from God, from others, from ourselves! When Adam and Eve knew that they were sinners, they sewed fig leaves together to make protective covering not only to hide their nakedness from each other, but to hide themselves from God. They hoped God would not notice that they were changed.

We who are descended from Adam and Eve and inherit a sinful nature from them do the same thing: We create impenetrable defenses to protect our hearts from being known! We say to ourselves (consciously or unconsciously), "I don't want anyone to know me - to really know me. I'll let them know the person I create that is safe for me to have them know. But I will wear a mask to guard myself from being too deeply known."

We don't trust anyone with the kind of knowledge Psalm 139 attributes to God. It doesn't feel safe to be known like that. And we instinctively take this posture toward God:

> *"Ah, you who hide deep from the LORD your counsel, whose deeds are in the dark, and who say, 'Who sees us? Who knows us?' You turn things upside down! Shall the potter be regarded as the clay, that the thing made should say of its maker, 'He did not make me'; or the thing formed say of him who formed it, 'He has no understanding'?"* (Isaiah 29:15-16)

To experience a deep, honest relationship with God, you have to confess that you can't escape God's knowledge of you, you can't hide from him! You need to be honest with God about what's in your heart.

No need to fear

God knows everything about you. You might as well be honest with him about what you're thinking and feeling! You can welcome his knowledge of you or you can resist the idea that God knows you like that.

But this is what the Scriptures affirm: God is not against you. He is for you! He is not your adversary. His motivation in knowing you completely is love.

"What then shall we say to these things? If God is for us, who can be against us? He who did not spare his own Son but gave him up for us all, how will he not also with him give us all things...For I am sure that neither death nor life, nor angels nor rulers, nor things present nor things to come, nor powers, nor height nor depth, nor anything else in all creation, will be able to separate us from the love of God in Christ Jesus our Lord" (Romans 8:31-32, 38-39).

You don't have to be afraid of what God will find when he searches your heart. He already knows what is there, and still loves you. God doesn't need to be informed about what's in your heart, but you do! You don't understand what is driving you in the choices you make and the words you say every day. There are depths to your heart and soul that you don't understand. For God to show you the truth about the sin that is driving your heart is a good thing. Sin always creates bondage. To the degree your words and actions are driven by sinful assumptions and motives, you are not free. God wants you to experience real freedom. But you can't experience that freedom until you begin to see what is there in your heart.

So what if you pray, *"Search me, O God, and know my heart! Try me and know my thoughts! And see if there be any grievous way in me, and lead me in the way everlasting."*

What would it look like for God to answer that prayer? How would God show you what he wants you to see about what's going on in your heart?

He might give you insight into your sin as you pray or as you read Scripture alone in your times with him. He might make you aware of something you need to confess and show you where you need repentance. He might stir your conscience without anyone else being involved. But usually, we need some help to see what's in our hearts. Would you be willing to hear what God might say to you about the sinful motives, desires, or patterns in your heart through another person?

Those who are closest to you know some things about how you sin that you may not see for yourself. Your wife, your husband, your parents, your child, an honest friend – would you be willing to believe that God might show you your sin through someone close to you?

You say, "Willing? Maybe if I can't avoid it. But I am not about to seek out that kind of scrutiny! I don't want to hear someone's thoughts about my failings. It's too painful! It tears down what I've been trying to believe all my life: All my life I've been trying to do for myself what needs to be done, to do it by myself, and to do it as quickly as possible! To hear that someone sees imperfections is painful!" We would never say it, but what we think is: "I want to be perfect, or at least reasonably and consistently super-adequate!"

Trying to hide

In a very helpful book, *The Trauma of Transparency*, the author says:

"I want to be perfect. I know I'm not. So I hide my imperfections. From whom? Well, there are a lot of things that are true about me that I either don't know about or won't admit to myself. I hide from myself! I hide from others. I hide from God! ...when will I stop hiding?"

The answer is:

"I'll stop hiding when I'm perfect! Then it will be safe and easy to be open and honest with everyone, all the time, about anything. I'll have nothing to hide. But that isn't going to happen in this life on this earth! So we keep hiding....refusing to face what we need to deal with!" (J. Grant Howard, p.41-42).

You can keep hiding from others, but you can't hide from God. Because he loves you, he wants what is best for you – he wants you to be free from the sinful assumptions, beliefs, motives, and actions that enslave you. So he is going to expose your sin in one way or another. It is only when you see your sin and are made aware of your inability to change your own heart that you will run to Jesus for grace. And to know the depths of the love God has for you, you need to see what Jesus did for you on the cross more clearly! You need to see the enormity of God's work of grace for you in Christ's suffering and death in your place.

If you can believe that God exposes your sin because he loves you, you will be more willing to pray, *"Search me and know me..."*

What if, after you said some unloving or angry words to someone you loved, you calmed down enough to really consider what just happened? What if you prayed, "Father, where is the truth in this? Would you show me what I need to see about my heart and give me the grace to change?"

What if you prayed, "Father, work in me, change me, set me free from the bondage of sin that remains in me. I don't understand why I do this and act like this and I feel so unsafe for you to know me like I really am. But you chose me in love. You adopted me as your child. You've promised you will not reject me or hide from me. Give me the grace to trust you to show me my sin and clean up my heart."

Those kinds of honest, deep, heartfelt prayers can change your life.

Ask God to search your heart

When Jesus taught his disciples to pray, *"Hallowed be your name,"* what did he have in mind? It's valid to pray that God's name would he held in honor (hallowed) by people in your town or in our nation. It's a good thing to ask that people in cultures and tribes and nations who don't know Jesus as Savior and Lord would come to hallow God's name. But what about God's name being hallowed in your heart and mind? We need God's Spirit to show us where we don't honor God in our hearts. We need God to show us the truth about our sinful desires, motives, attitudes and assumptions.

Asking God to search your heart and to know you is asking God to hallow His name in your life. "Lord, show me your holiness, that I might see the depths of my sin more clearly. And don't leave me there, but show me how the work of Jesus on the cross is sufficient to bridge the vast chasm that distances me from you. Only as I see your holiness more clearly and long for your name to be hallowed in my life will I face the truth about the depths of sin in my heart. If I refuse to face the truth about what is driving my heart, I will not value your mercy in Christ highly enough."

Coming to God with this kind of honesty, inviting his search of your heart and asking him to show you any offensive way that is in you opens you up to a deeper understanding of yourself. That, in turn, leads to a greater intimacy with Jesus, the "lover of your soul!"

Chapter 5

THINK Before You Pray

PSALM 1 IS A PREFACE TO THE BOOK OF PSALMS. It's the door into the world of psalms and sets the stage for all the psalms.

Psalm 1: *Blessed is the man who walks not in the counsel of the wicked, nor stands in the way of sinners, nor sits in the seat of scoffers; 2 but his delight is in the law of the LORD, and on his law he meditates day and night. 3 He is like a tree planted by streams of water that yields its fruit in its season, and its leaf does not wither. In all that he does, he prospers. 4 The wicked are not so, but are like chaff that the wind drives away. 5 Therefore the wicked will not stand in the judgment, nor sinners in the congregation of the righteous; 6 for the LORD knows the way of the righteous, but the way of the wicked shall perish.*

Psalm 1 describes a person who meditates on God's law day and night. Meditation is something we usually associate with new age religions or Buddhism. But meditation has an important place in Christian prayer. The psalms encourage meditation in two directions: pondering God's words and pondering God's works. Christian meditation involves choosing what your mind will ponder.

In this chapter we will focus on meditation on God's words. In the next, we'll consider meditation on God's works.

The psalm sets before us a contrast between two ways: the way of the righteous versus the way of the wicked. It is important to note it is not about someone who is righteous because he works hard to keep all God's commandments and actually pulls it off.

"Righteous" is a category meaning "one who is right with God." "Wicked" is the contrasting category. It's a term we don't use much, which was clear to me when I highlighted the word in Microsoft Word and looked up "synonyms." For words that mean the same thing as "wicked" I was given: good, great, outstanding, amazing, cool, fabulous! My kids talk like that sometimes: "That roller coaster was really wicked!"

In the Bible, the word "wicked" is a behavioral term that means evil. Something that is wicked is morally wrong. More specifically, it is a pattern of life set in opposition to God.

The "righteous" and the "wicked" are contrasted throughout the Psalms. The psalmists explain there are two ways you can choose: the way of life or the way of death. In other words, there are two paths you can follow in your life: a righteous path or a wicked path.

One way produces stability that will outlast this life (like a tree planted by streams of water). The other way produces a life that is inherently unstable, like chaff the wind blows away. When grain was harvested in days before machines, wheat was put in a basket and tossed in the air. The grain was heavier than the husk, so the shell, the grassy part of the plant, would blow away in the wind while the kernel of wheat fell back into the basket. The worthless part that blew away was called "chaff." It wasn't wanted, it was useless and not heavy enough to last. It simply blew away with the wind. That's what the way of the wicked is like. Instead of stability like a tree planted by nourishing water, it just blows away worthless, like it never mattered. Saying the way of the wicked will "perish" does not only mean physical death, but spiritual death, eternal death. The contrast is eternally profound.

Blessed is the man

What does it mean to be blessed?

Some Bible translations say, *"Happy is the man..."* Maybe they thought the word "blessed" was outdated, but its meaning is much richer than what we mean by "happy!" To be happy means you feel good, you're in a good mood, things are going great. You are happy when your problems are small. You're happy when you're not sad. "Happy" describes your experience at some point in time. Because you're having a good time, you feel happy. When things are not going well or your problems increase, you become unhappy.

But to be blessed by God, in biblical terms, is to have God's affirmation resting on you:

"The LORD bless you...The LORD make his face to shine upon you and be gracious to you..." (Numbers 6:24-26).

Being blessed by God doesn't depend on how you're feeling. You can be going through tough times, times of disappointment, times full of sorrow, times of emotional or physical pain, times when you don't particularly feel very happy, and still have God's blessing on your life. To be blessed is to have God's smile of approval on you because you are united by God's grace to Jesus Christ. You are blessed when the guilt of your sin is forgiven and you are adopted as God's son or daughter. That is a condition that outlasts this present life; *"a tree planted by streams of water."*

The blessed person of Psalm 1 is also called *"the righteous."* It means someone who has chosen to live under God's Word, trusting God, pursuing God, and is right with God through faith in God's saving grace. You can read back into this psalm what it means to be right before God through the justifying grace of Jesus Christ:

"For I am not ashamed of the gospel, for it is the power of God for salvation to everyone who believes, to the Jew first and also to the Greek. For in it the righteousness of God is revealed from faith for faith, as it is written, 'The righteous shall live by faith'" (Romans 1:16-17).

That isn't just a New Testament idea. It was there in the Old Testament, though certainly made more clear with the coming of Christ. We need righteousness. We don't have it in ourselves. But God provides atonement for us, and gives us the grace to believe Him, to trust Him. To be right with God through his saving grace in Jesus Christ is what it means to be blessed.

Now look at the progression: *Blessed is the man who does not....walk, stand, sit.*

A treacherous walk

Imagine you're walking down the street, and you pass an outdoor café. You see people eating and talking. The smell of good cooking invades your nostrils and you stop walking. You walk over to the door and stand there to read the menu! And pretty soon, you're sitting at a table ordering something good for lunch.

That's a pretty harmless progression. But it's not a café offering harmless good food here in Psalm 1. It's a purposeful, knowing, downward progression leading directly to *"the counsel of the wicked."* This is not an innocent walk. It's a walk down a road leading directly to people, places, thoughts, and actions in direct opposition to God. It's a chosen path leading directly to wickedness.

Again, "wicked" means evil. More specifically, morally evil. It is a way of living that is opposed to what God says is right and true. The counsel of the wicked is everyone and everything set in opposition to God and to what he says is good and true and right.

You can't stop living in this world when you become a Christian. You can't protect your children from the counsel of the wicked by homeschooling or sending them to a Christian School or getting rid of the television. We are surrounded by the pervasive attitude of fallen people. To some degree you can't help but be around the counsel of the wicked. But you don't have to purposefully walk directly into it.

So often we don't even think about what we're letting influence our minds and hearts. We think so many things in our culture are harmless. But there is no neutral position in all this. There are only two ways: one thinks it can define good and bad, right and wrong, true and false without any reference to God or His Word. The other defines good and bad, right and wrong, true and false in light of God's revelation in

His written Word.

Follow the progression

It begins with a walk.

As has already been stated, this is a purposeful walk leading directly to a place you know you don't belong – a place where ungodly thoughts, actions, and ideas are found. It's a walk which takes you to the "counsel of the wicked." For you are no longer even walking.

You stand.

The "way" of the wicked has now moved to the next level as you *"stand in the way of sinners."* Standing gives you the opportunity to really observe and take it all in. You're close enough to see everything for yourself. The psalmist says, you are now *"standing in the way of sinners."*

As you stand, you listen to the thoughts, ideas, mindset, and views of the counsel of the wicked. The people sitting in this counsel seem quite typical and don't appear all that offensive. In fact, the more you listen, the more normal, good, and appealing it all seems.

You sit down.

The third step in the progression has just been reached. You are now *"sitting in the seat of scoffers."* "Scoffers" are those who mock what God says. They say "it's stupid and unrealistic to live the way God commands." They say it takes the fun out of life and it's ridiculous to believe what God says in the Bible. They say God's moral views and opinions about what is true or false are outdated and irrelevant to the modern world.

In the psalms, "the wicked" refers to people who defiantly choose a path that is contrary to what God commands. The most hardened people are the ones sitting – the mockers and scoffers – who are proud in their opinion that it's stupid to believe what the Bible says or to build your life around God. This is the place where ungodly thoughts, ideas and actions are presented as wisdom – as good counsel. It is a place where thoughts, deeds and actions are set against God himself.

The wicked's end

But *the way of the wicked will perish* (vs. 6). The "way" refers to the course of life, the pattern of life, the choices and behavior, and finally, to the consequences of living life opposed to God. The way of the wicked is a trajectory of life with an inevitable destiny.

So the psalm warns people who want to live under God's blessing to avoid the downward spiral that starts with setting foot on this path: from thinking like those set against God, to choosing a godless lifestyle, to being at home with a godless life. Don't even start on this path!

The blessed path

Why does the blessed person not go that way? Because *"his delight is in the law of the LORD."* The reason he chooses not to go down the path of the wicked is that his heart delights in something completely different and his mind is preoccupied with different thoughts: *"On His law he meditates day and night."*

On the surface, "meditating on God's laws day and night" doesn't necessarily sound motivating. But what does it really mean? Meditating on God's "law" means so much more than just thinking about the moral law of God summarized in the Ten Commandments. For Old Testament believers, every word of Scripture was the law of God. The psalmist is saying, then, the righteous man meditates on the entire written Word of God.

Meditating on God's law is to think and focus on what God has revealed about himself. It is to delight the structure God has given which points us to Christ and sets us free from the enslaving power of sin. And because this is where his mind and heart are centered, the result in his life is described in verse 3: *"like a tree planted by a stream"* drawing refreshing strength from God's Word.

In other words, the person who meditates on God's Word doesn't dry up and become fruitless. In all he does, he prospers. That doesn't mean he never has setbacks or difficulties, but in the course of his life, he has chosen what is eternal, what is best – he has set his heart on a treasure that can never be lost! The trajectory of his life is toward God and life under God's blessing.

In contrast, the wicked are like chaff that the wind blows away. They won't stand up in the judgment. They won't have a place with the redeemed people of God. The wicked will perish in the end.

The Psalms develop these truths in lots of ways and expand on these basic ideas. As you read through the Psalms, notice how often the way of the righteous and the way of the wicked are contrasted. But let's focus on what is said in verse 2: *"His delight is in the law of the LORD, and on his law he meditates day and night."*

Meditate?

The idea of meditating is a bit foreign to us. What comes to mind when you read the word, "meditation?" Maybe you think of religions that talk a lot about meditation: Buddhism, Transcendental Meditation (TM), New Age religions that have grown out of Buddhist ideas. In those religions, the goal of meditation is to stop thinking, to clear your mind of all thought. Suppose you have a problem or are full of sorrow. The way to find peace is to clear your mind of all thought. Buddhism tells you to think of life as an illusion – the pain isn't real. Meditation is about learning techniques for calming your anxious heart by not thinking.

Have you ever tried to think of nothing? There are times when I sit on the sofa quietly, and my wife says, "What are you thinking about?" I respond, "Oh, nothing." I don't mean that my mind has been completely blank and no thoughts have been going through my head. I mean I've not been thinking of anything important or anything I want to talk about. It's almost impossible to think of nothing! Something is going through your mind all the time!

The word, "amusement" comes from the root word to muse, which means to think. The letter "a" added to "muse" makes it a negative: to not think. But something is going on in your mind when you are watching a DVD or playing a video game. Your mind isn't completely blank! You don't stop thinking completely. It's just that what you're thinking about is a diversion from the daily routine. In that sense, amusement is a diversion that gets certain thoughts off your mind by allowing you to think about something different, something light-hearted or compelling enough to allow you to not think about the things that normally occupy your mind.

When the psalms encourage us to meditate on God's law, they are encouraging us to choose what our minds will ponder. It is interesting how often the idea of meditation comes up in the psalms:

> *"I will meditate on your precepts and fix my eyes on your ways. I will delight in your statutes; I will not forget your word... – your servant will meditate on your statutes..."* (Psalm 119:15-16, 23).

> *"Oh how I love your law! It is my meditation all the day..."* (Psalm 119:97).

> *"...your testimonies are my meditation..."* (Psalm 119:99).

The psalmists tell God they delight in meditating. For a Christian, this means reflecting on what is true about the universe in light of what God has said in his Word and what he has revealed and accomplished in Jesus Christ. In the terminology of Psalm 1, since your mind is always occupied with something, choose to saturate your mind and heart with God's thoughts. In 1 Corinthians the Apostle Paul encourages the same thing when he says, *"We impart this in words not taught by human wisdom but taught by the Spirit..."* (see I Corinthians 2:5 and 2:13).

Meditate on this

Many of the Psalms are prayers, but they are also meditations in which the psalmist ponders some aspect of the character of God. For example, Psalm 139 ponders the intimate knowledge God has of each of us: *"O LORD, you have searched me and known me...before a word is on my tongue, you know it altogether..."* He is pondering these things before God in prayer, talking to God about what amazes him about God's knowledge.

Again, Psalm 1 tells us the righteous man meditates day and night on God's law. He rolls things around in his mind as he works, as he walks down the road, when he wakes up in the morning, and when he lies down to sleep at night. He's thinking about God's Word, which means he's thinking about what God has revealed about himself. He is pondering what it means to relate to God, to be loved by God, to be known by God, to belong to God's covenant people, to experience God's tender mercy and steadfast love, and much more – *"His delight is in the law of the LORD, and on his law he meditates day and night."*

Learning to pray

People sometimes ask me, "What should I talk about when I pray?" They usually tell me, "I end up asking God for things I need. I confess my sin, ask him to forgive me. But then what?" What they are really asking is, "How do I learn to enjoy talking to God so it doesn't feel like a boring duty? How can prayer become a delight?"

First, think about how you grow to enjoy talking to anyone. You have to want to get to know that person. You have to be interested enough in what he thinks to ask him questions and listen to what matters to him. And you have to choose to spend time with him.

Prayer involves your mind. It requires thinking. You have to want to know about the God to whom you speak. And God has made himself known in his Word. So prayer flows out of a growing awareness of who God is and what he has said about himself. Maybe that's why the psalmist says he meditates on God's Word. You can't really know God apart from what he has said about himself in Scripture. You can know certain things must be true about God by observing the world around you. But to know God, you have to learn what he tells you about himself.

Prayer involves your heart. You can "pray" out of a sense of duty – because you know you're supposed to pray. But if you talked to your wife because it was your duty to spend a little time every day talking to her, how would she respond? She wants to know that you are interested in her, that you want to know her and listen to what is on her heart. In a similar way, prayer becomes a delight when you really desire God, when you are hungry and thirsty for God.

Prayer involves your will. It means choosing to spend time this way and training yourself to tell God what is on your mind and heart. Prayer becomes more of a delight as you learn to live with an awareness of being in God's presence all the time. The more we meditate on his Word and get to know him, the more delight we experience in our thoughts, prayers, and life.

Some Practical Suggestions:
1. **Meditation requires content (...on his law he meditates...).**

    If you're going to meditate on God's Word, you need to actually get some part of his Word before your mind to think about! There is no command in the Bible about when you should read your Bible (morning or evening) or how much Scripture you should read. There are times when it's good to read a large section, maybe even a whole letter like Galatians or Colossians at one sitting. (These were, after all, letters, meant to be read completely, not little by little). But there are other times for taking just a few words as the subject of meditation.

    With all the technological advances in our day, you can listen to someone reading Scripture on your computer or smartphone. Just find a way to get some portion of God's Word before your mind. As you listen or as you read, ask yourself, "What does this passage tell me about God? According to this passage, what is God like?" Instead of guessing about what God is like, let his Word inform your thoughts about God.

2. **If you're going to ponder what you've just read or heard, you can't let other thoughts occupy your mind.**

    This is hard for a lot of people in our generation to believe, but I can assure you it's true: silence is okay! You're actually going to need some silence if you're going to let your mind ponder the truth you've just read or heard from God's Word.

    It helps to minimize distractions. My dad could sit in a room with people talking and read a book. He could tune out all the noise and think about what he was reading. But if you turned on the television, his attention was drawn to the TV. It distracted him enough that he couldn't think with the TV on.

    Some people seem to be able to read and think with music playing or with the television on. People say, "It's just background noise. I tune it out." I've never been able to do that, especially if the music in the background is something I know, or if it's jazz music.

I need silence, without distractions, if I'm going to mull over things I've read in the Bible. I find some of my best time for reflecting on what I've read in Scripture is when I'm alone in the car or when I'm mowing the lawn. I don't listen to music in the car. I have learned to enjoy the silence because it gives me time to think. And I've learned to turn my thoughts toward God and to talk to God about what he has said about himself in Scripture.

Your prayers don't have to be long or carefully worded. You can tell God what you're thinking about or that you have a hard time understanding something you read in the Bible. Tell him that you want to know him and delight in him.

3. **If you're going to meditate on God's Word, should you have set times or should it be spontaneous?**

The answer is "Yes." The psalmist talks about reflecting on God's Word in the morning and in the evening, when he gets up, when he walks down the road, and when he lies down at night.

You need to know yourself well enough to choose the times when your mind works best. For some people, that's early in the morning. But that's not true for everyone. Other people function better late at night.

Set times are great and building those times into your schedule is wise. If you don't set times for reading scripture and for meditation, other things will take up your time. But on the other hand, a good suggestion is to take advantage of some of those times usually filled with television or other forms of amusement.

What about the time you spend every day commuting to work? If you have a drive to work, instead of listening to music on the radio, listen to a sermon or to a passage of Scripture. This can be an excellent use of your smart phone or CD player. But here's the key, listen, then turn it off and ponder what you just heard. Make it a time of reflection and prayer.

What about when you mow the lawn? Instead of putting on headphones and listening to music, what if you read a section of Scripture before you started the lawnmower, and then pondered that passage as you mowed the lawn?

What about taking a little time before you go to sleep to read something from God's Word and then ponder those words before you fall asleep?

4. **Pray before meditation: Ask God:** *"open my eyes that I may see wonderful things in your word and get to know you better."*
5. **Learn to ask questions of the passage of Scripture you are reading.**
    For example, as you read Psalm 1, you can ask:
    Why will the wicked *not* stand?
    Why do the righteous flourish?
    What would it mean for me to be like a tree planted by a stream, a tree that produces fruit and doesn't wither?
    What does it mean to be blessed by God?
    How do I tend to follow that downward spiral: walking in the way, standing, sitting – where do I tend to do that?

What does it mean to be one of the righteous who stays away from the path of the wicked?

Based on all this, what do I need to say to God? What do I need to ask him to do in my heart? Where do I need his grace to lead me to Jesus in repentance and faith?

Think

Ask questions of the passage. Then ask God to give you insight. Pray God's Word back to him! Thomas Watson said: "Study is the finding out of a truth, meditation is the spiritual improvement of a truth; the one searches for the vein of gold, the other digs out the gold."

After meditation you have something to pray about! You can say: "Father, I've been thinking about what you said. This is what I see more clearly about what you are like. This is what I don't understand. This is what I see more clearly about myself.

This is what gives me joy…"

The Puritan pastor, Thomas Manton, said: "The Word feeds meditation, and meditation feeds prayer." If this is a new idea for you – if you're not used to taking some time to reflect and ponder a portion of Scripture or some words from a passage you've been reading, it is going to be like trying to build a fire with wet wood. It will take some time! But stay after it! Ask the Holy Spirit to help you focus on what this passage tells you about God. Ask him to help you focus your mind and heart on the glory of God in the face of Jesus Christ.

What you think about, what you ponder, the content of your musing, reveals what matters to you. Someone said: "If farmers think about their land and crops; if doctors think about patients they want to help; if lawyers think about their latest cases; if store owners think about how they can sell more; shouldn't the minds of Christians be drawn to contemplation of the truth about God our Savior?"

What you will find as you take the time to meditate on God's Word and talk to him about what you are finding in his Word is that God himself will become a delight to your soul!

Chapter 6

Talk to God about What He has Done

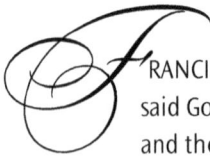

FRANCIS BACON (1561-1626), the English statesman and scientist, said God has given us two books or volumes to study: the scriptures and the natural realm. To know God, he said, we need both books. The Bible reveals the will of God, but to understand the greatness of the God who has revealed himself in the Bible, we need to be drawn into thoughtful reflection on the infinite power of God, which is seen most clearly in his works.

Along with commands to meditate on God's words in Scripture, the psalms invite us to ponder the works of God:

> *"I will extol you, my God and King, and bless your name forever and ever. Every day I will bless you and praise your name forever and ever. Great is the LORD, and greatly to be praised, and his greatness is unsearchable. One generation shall commend your works to another, and shall declare your mighty acts. On the glorious splendor of your majesty, and on your wondrous works, I will meditate"* (Psalm 145:1-5).

Meditating on God's works would include pondering God's work in creation, his daily care for all he has made, and his works of redemption that are recounted in the Bible.

God's Handiwork on Display

On a clear day, the white ice fields and glaciers of coastal Alaska seem endless as you gaze out the window of an airplane heading from Seattle to Anchorage. Up close, the blue and green colors of the ice sparkle as huge chunks of ice calve off the end of the glacier and crash into the sea. The beauty of glaciers and their power to carve channels through mountains is impressive. But you can look at all that beauty and power, be impressed, and still miss something significant!

In the summer of 1881, the American naturalist, John Muir spent three months exploring and mapping what is now Glacier Bay. His traveling companion was Samuel Young, a Presbyterian missionary. Muir was a Christian. He saw God's glory, power and majesty everywhere in the natural realm, and his delight in God is refreshing (his account is available in a book entitled *Travels in Alaska*).

After an exhilarating day exploring a glacier, Muir wrote that he came down the mountain, "rejoicing in the possession of so blessed a day, and feeling that in very foundational truth we had been in one of God's own temples and had seen him and heard him working and preaching like a man." He described an unusual display of Northern Lights as the Word of God in "majestic hieroglyphics blazoned along the sky."

When Muir explored glaciers, he saw more than massive rivers of ice. He described a glacier as a window into God's ongoing work of creation: Valleys are being carved for new rivers, basins are being hollowed out for lakes, soil that will feed new forests is being ground by the slow moving ice, and the silt that flows out to the ocean is slowly built into beautiful new mountains and landscapes that God has long planned.

To see the world this way, to know that the God who created such majesty and beauty is still at work in what we see around us should move us to doxology – to praising God. God tells us about his power and glory in the majesty of the world around us clearly and powerfully. And it's on display daily!

Muir's advice to his missionary friend is also good advice for us today:

"Keep close to Nature's heart, yourself; and break clear away, once in a while, and climb a mountain or spend a week in the woods. Wash your spirit clean from the earth-stains of this sordid, gold-seeking crowd in God's pure air. It will help you in your efforts to bring to these men something better than gold. Don't lose your freedom and your love of the Earth as God made it."

That's good advice. Get outside. Open your eyes and look at what God has made. Consider the wisdom and power required to make the things you see in the heavens and in the world around you. If the world God has made is magnificent and beautiful, what must the Creator be like?

A scientist by the name of Charles Misner, a specialist in general relativity theory, said:

"I do see the design of the universe as essentially a religious question. That is, one should have some kind of respect and awe for the whole business… It's very magnificent and shouldn't be taken for granted. In fact, I believe that is why Einstein had so little use for organized religion, although he strikes me as a basically very religious man. He must have looked at what the preachers said about God and felt that they were blaspheming. He had seen much more majesty than they had ever imagined, and they were just not talking about the real thing. My guess is that he simply felt that religions he'd run across did not have proper respect…for the author of the universe" (John Piper, *Think*, p.194).

What Einstein didn't know

Misner could be right, but his critique may not be a completely fair assessment of the God presented by Christians or of Einstein's religious leanings. Einstein's religion, according to Einstein, was "a knowledge of the existence of something we cannot penetrate, of the manifestations of the profoundest reason and the most radiant beauty – it is this knowledge and this emotion that constitute the truly religious attitude; in this sense, and in this alone, I am a deeply religious man."

His comprehension of the infinite vastness of space created a deep sense of wonder and awe. He couldn't explain how the universe began, how it was organized so perfectly, or why it was so beautiful. Through his understanding of math and his observations of the planets and stars and galaxies through telescopes, Einstein knew something of the vastness of space and the order and design was impossible to deny. It filled him with wonder and awe. His sense of amazement felt like a kind of devotion.

But if you are amazed at something beautiful and want to express praise, to whom do you direct those feelings and expressions of adoration? Einstein didn't know!

He sometimes spoke of God in ways that resonate with Christians. For example:

"We are in the position of a little child entering a huge library filled with books in many different languages. The child knows someone must have written those books. It does not know how. It does not understand the languages in which they are written. The child dimly suspects a mysterious order in the arrangement of the books but doesn't know what it is. That, it seems to me, is the attitude of even the most intelligent human being toward God. We see a universe marvelously arranged and obeying certain laws, but only dimly understand these laws. Our limited minds cannot grasp the mysterious force that moves the constellations."

It's as if he could sense the presence and power of God, but was unable to take the next step and acknowledge the reality and existence of the God of the Bible:

"I do not believe in a personal God and I have never denied this but have expressed it clearly. If something is in me which can be called religious then it is the unbounded admiration for the structure of the world so far as our science can reveal it."

He said, "I believe in Spinoza's God who reveals himself in the orderly harmony of what exists, not in a God who concerns himself with the fates and actions of human beings."

In his attempts to appreciate the greatness and majesty of God that he could see in creation, Einstein actually made God small by limiting him and refusing to believe that God is a person who wants to be known. If there is a God who spoke and called the universe into being, he would have to be greater than the universe he made, and the universe appears to be infinite. But, he thought, how could a God of that kind of vastness and power be knowable? And why would a God like that care about one little planet or one particular species on that planet or one little person on that planet?

We would do well to ponder the vastness of the universe, like Einstein did. We have Hubble Telescope pictures and information about distant galaxies that he never saw through his telescopes. We would do well to feel the sense of mystery he felt when he thought about the kind of power it would take to make something so infinitely vast and fill it with planets and stars. Maybe we do need a greater respect for the author of the universe.

Is God too big and majestic to know me?

At the same time, we should ponder the mystery of God's loving care for human beings. It's not an either/or thing. The God we worship is infinitely powerful, gloriously majestic, and at the same time, personal and knowable.

> *"To whom then will you compare me, that I should be like him? Says the Holy One. Lift up your eyes on high and see; who created these? He who brings out their host by number, calling them all by name, by the greatness of his might, and because he is strong in power not one is missing"* (Isaiah 40:25-26).

God himself encourages us to ponder the universe when we need a sense of the greatness of God.

> But He goes on to say, *"Why do you say, O Jacob, and speak, O Israel, 'My way is hidden from the LORD, and my right is disregarded by my God'?"* (Isaiah 40:27).

There it is! The God who made and sustains the universe is fully aware of what's going on in our lives. He cares about people like us! He is big enough to create and sustain the entire universe. But he's not so busy running the universe that he can't stoop to care for one tiny planet in a remote solar system. And this majestic God, who made all that exists, is the one who makes himself known to us in Jesus Christ and invites us into relationship with himself.

Now that is something to ponder!

How would a greater awareness of the world around you move you to respond to God? If our talk about God does not stir up a deeper sense of wonder and awe and reverence and respect for God, something is wrong. And if our prayers do not have some sense of wonder and awe and respect and reverence for the greatness and majesty of God, how aware are we of who God is?

In the last chapter, we looked at meditation on the words of God in Scripture. As someone who has been delivered from the dominion of darkness and brought into the kingdom of the Lord Jesus, God's Word increasingly becomes a delight because it reveals God. You can't love someone you don't know. God wants you to know him. He has made Jesus known to you, he has made himself known to you through the written testimony of the Bible. To meditate on God's Word is to ponder what God has said in Scripture so as to get the truth into your heart, so you will delight in Christ and be moved to deeper love for Christ.

Meditate on God's works

But the psalms also encourage us to meditate on God's works.

What you find repeatedly in the psalms is a sense of wonder and delight in the majesty of God stirred up by a due consideration or meditation on the works of God. And if the psalms are going to teach us something about prayer, it would be good for us to pay attention to this.

"I will extol you, my God and King, and bless your name forever and ever. Every day I will bless you and praise your name forever and ever. Great is the LORD, and greatly to be praised, and his greatness is unsearchable.

"One generation shall commend your works to another, and shall declare your mighty acts. On the glorious splendor of your majesty, and on your wondrous works, I will meditate. They shall speak of the might of your awesome deeds, and I will declare your greatness. They shall pour forth the fame of your abundant goodness and shall sing aloud of your righteousness.

"The LORD is gracious and merciful, slow to anger and abounding in steadfast love. The LORD is good to all, and his mercy is over all that he has made.

"All your works shall give thanks to you, O LORD, and all your saints shall bless you! They shall speak of the glory of your kingdom and tell of your power, to make known to the children of man your mighty deeds, and the glorious splendor of your kingdom. Your kingdom is an everlasting kingdom, and your dominion endures throughout all generations.

"[The LORD is faithful in all his words and kind in all his works.]

"The LORD upholds all who are falling and raises up all who are bowed down. The eyes of all look to you, and you give them their food in due season. You open your hand; you satisfy the desire of every living thing. The LORD is righteous in all his ways and kind in all his works. The LORD is near to all who call on him, to all who call on him in truth. He fulfills the desire of those who fear him; he also hears their cry and saves them. The LORD preserves all who love him, but all the wicked he will destroy.

"My mouth will speak the praise of the LORD, and let all flesh bless his holy name forever and ever" (Psalm 145).

"When I look at your heavens, the work of your fingers, the moon and the stars, which you have set in place" (Psalm 8:3).

On the Hubble Telescope website there is a link to the "Hubble Deep Field." Astronomers saw what looked like a dark space in the heavens, empty of stars. With the Hubble Telescope, they were able to focus on that dark area and expose film for thirty to forty minutes. What they found astounded them. What seemed to be an empty, dark spot was actually filled with distant spinning galaxies. Their conclusion is that there is no empty space. No matter which direction they focus telescopes, there are stars and planets. Some are just so far away that they appear to our eyes, even through telescopes, as empty, dark spaces.

Our vast galaxy

Light travels at the speed of 5.87 trillion miles a year. The galaxy of which our solar system is a part is about 100,000 light-years in diameter – about 587 thousand trillion miles. It is one of about a million such galaxies in the optical range of our most powerful telescopes. In our galaxy there are about 100 billion stars. The sun around which our planet travels is just one of the many stars in our galaxy – a modest little star burning at about 6,000 degrees centigrade on the surface and traveling in an orbit at 155 miles per second, which means it will take about 200 million years to compete one revolution around the galaxy. And our galaxy is one of millions. How do you begin to comprehend those kinds of complexities or the vastness of the universe?

Considering some of the pictures we have received from the Hubble Telescope, Dallas Willard wrote:

"A short while ago the Hubble Space Telescope gave us pictures of the Eagle Nebula, showing clouds of gas and microscopic dust reaching six trillion miles from top to bottom. Hundreds of stars were emerging here and there in it, hotter and larger than our sun... Human beings can lose themselves in card games or electric trains and think they are fortunate. But to God there is available... 'Towering clouds of gases trillions of miles high, backlit by nuclear fires in newly forming stars, galaxies cartwheeling into collision and sending explosive shock waves boiling through millions of light years of time and space.' These things are all before him, along with numberless unfolding rosebuds, souls, and songs – and immeasurably more of which we know nothing" (*The Divine Conspiracy,* p. 63-64).

Think of it: the God who made all this and holds it together moment by moment, is the God who has revealed himself as a loving and personal God who wants a relationship with you! He upholds the universe, but he also cares about you.

God's Works of Redemption

"O LORD, our Lord, how majestic is your name in the all the earth! You have set your glory above the heavens. Out of the mouth of babes and infants, you have established strength because of your foes, to still the enemy and the avenger.

"When I look at your heavens, the work of your fingers, the moon and the stars, which you have set in place, what is man that you are mindful of him, and the son of man that you care for him? Yet you have made him a little lower than the heavenly beings and crowned him with glory and honor.

"You have given him dominion over the works of your hands; you have put all things under his feet, all sheep and oxen, and also the beasts of the field, the birds of the heavens, and the fish of the sea, whatever passes along the paths of the seas. O LORD, our Lord, how majestic is your name in all the earth!" (Psalm 8)

If God is infinitely powerful, which he would have to be to uphold the universe, and if God could speak and call into being all that exists, he would have to be greater than the universe he created. The universe appears to be infinite: it has no end.

Pondering that vastness, we feel small. Why would a God like that want to know us? Why would he care about our lives and concerns? For reasons we will never comprehend, God chose to make human beings in his own image and likeness because he wanted to lavish love on us. He made us for a relationship with himself. It's mind boggling, but he wants us to know him and delight in him.

We who have come to faith in Jesus Christ, who have been drawn into a relationship with the living God, the Creator and Sustainer of all things should be the most awed by the majesty and grandeur and greatness of God! We believe that the God who made all that exists is knowable and personal. He has demonstrated clearly in his works of redemption (recounted in the whole Bible) that he wants a relationship with us – a Father-child relationship of love!

"Give thanks to the LORD, for he is good, for his steadfast love endures forever...to him who does great wonders...to him who by understanding made the heavens...to him who spread out the earth above the waters" (Psalm 136:1,5,6).

Those are God's works of creation. But the psalm goes on:

"...to him who struck down the firstborn of Egypt...and brought Israel out from among them" (Psalm 136:10).

Our Redeemer

From pondering God's works of creation with a sense of wonder and awe, the psalm moves to God's works of redemption. This infinitely wise and powerful God, who by understanding made the heavens and all that fills the heavens, this God who made the majestic planet on which we live, is the God who cares about human beings and moved in time and history to redeem a people from this fallen, sin-distorted world.

When the psalms talk about God's wonderful works, are they talking about marveling at the things God has made, or are they talking about the specific ways God acted on behalf of Israel? I think both are in view. We can praise God for his works in creation and praise him for his amazing display of love, power, mercy, patience and goodness in the way he has worked through the centuries as he has called and redeemed a people for his own glory.

"Give thanks unto the LORD, for He is good...O that men would praise the LORD for his goodness, and for his wonderful works to the children of men!" (Psalm 107:1,31).

Just to be clear: nature alone will not lead you to the truth about God. You can ponder the majesty of the world around you and not come to a deep understanding of who God is. That's why God gave us two books, as Francis Bacon put it. Ultimately, God has made himself known most clearly – he has spoken most clearly – in his Son, Jesus. If you really want to know what God is like, you need to ponder God's redeeming work that culminated in the cross of Christ. That is where you see the greatest display of God's wisdom, goodness, mercy and love. This is where you see God's condescending, tender mercy and his power to save!

Why did Jesus go to the cross? If the problems in our world could be solved by more education, better scientific methods, or greater advancements in technology, there would have been no need for God to send his Son into the world to suffer and die as a man. Our greatest problem is our alienation from God. Sin has brought ruin into the world in every dimension. Sin has distorted everything. So now we see beauty and majesty but live with brokenness and sadness. We live with a sense that things are not the way they should be.

Ponder God's works of redemption. God has made it clear: things are not the way they once were. But things are not now as they will be! God's work of redemption will bring about the restoration of this world when God is ready. Redemption is heading to a final, eternal glory. You find a longing for that eternal glory in your heart. God put it there. And it is by pondering the majesty of creation and the wonder of God's redeeming love that you put everything in proper perspective.

God's Works of Providence

God's works also include what theologians call his providence. God is holy, wise and powerful in the way he preserves and governs all the creatures he has made. You can ponder the way God has taken care of you through the days of life he has given you.

> *"Some went down to the sea in ships, doing business on the great waters; they saw the deeds of the LORD, his wondrous works in the deep. For he commanded and raised the stormy wind, which lifted up the waves of the sea.*

"They mounted up to heaven; they went down to the depths; their courage melted away in their evil plight; they reeled and staggered like drunken men and were at their wits end. Then they cried to the LORD in their trouble, and he delivered them from their distress.

"He made the storm be still, and the waves of the sea were hushed. Then they were glad that the waters were quiet, and he brought them to their desired haven. Let them thank the LORD for his steadfast love, for his wondrous works to the children of men! Let them extol him in the congregation of the people and praise him in the assembly of the elders" (Psalm 107:23-32).

Don't you wonder if the disciples of Jesus who saw him speak to the wind and waves and calm a storm at sea thought about this psalm and made the connection that Jesus did what only God can do? He spoke, and the wind stopped and the water grew glassy calm – instantly. Their question was: "Who is this that the wind and waves obey him?" You know the answer: He is the God described in Psalm 107.

How have you seen God's personal, fatherly care in your life? How have you seen the reality of God's works of providence? How have you seen God's goodness in your life? Can you tell him about it? Praise and thank him for his goodness?

"You have experienced the goodness of God every day of your life. Has this experience led you to repentance and faith in Christ? …Every meal, every pleasure, every possession, every bit of sun, every night's sleep, every moment of health and safety, everything else that sustains and enriches life, is a divine gift. And how abundant those gifts are!" (J.I. Packer, *Knowing God,* p. 147).

Where do you have a hard time seeing goodness in what God has allowed? How would pondering God's works among his people in the past encourage you to trust him?

If God knows each star and planet by name (and there are billions of them) why should you think that God doesn't know what's going on in your life, or that he is not capable of taking care of your needs? If God preserves the natural order daily, can you trust him to take care of you and of your family?

"Make me understand the way of your precepts, and I will meditate on your wondrous works" (Psalm 119:27).

What does all this have to do with prayer?

C.S. Lewis wrote:

"Pleasures are shafts of glory as it strikes our sensibility [our senses – we experience the world through taste, touch, smell, sight, and sound]…But aren't there bad, unlawful pleasures? Certainly there are. But in calling them 'bad pleasures' I take it we are using a kind of shorthand. We mean 'pleasures snatched by unlawful acts.' It is the stealing of the apples that is bad, not the sweetness. The sweetness is still a beam from the glory…I have tried since…to **make every pleasure into a channel of adoration.** I don't mean simply by giving thanks for it. One must of course give thanks, but I meant something different…Gratitude exclaims, very properly, 'How good of God to give me this.' Adoration says, 'What must be the quality of that Being whose far-off and momentary coruscations (flashes of light) are like this!' One's mind runs back up the sunbeam to the sun… If this is Hedonism, it is also a somewhat arduous discipline. But it is worth some labor."

Lewis is asking, if the short, sparkling glimpses we get of the beauty of God in the things he has made are wonderful, how much more beautiful and wonderful must God himself be? Lewis' advice is to make every pleasure a channel of adoration. Train yourself to thank and praise God for every beautiful thing you see, every pleasant taste you experience, and every beautiful sound you hear. Not only can you say, 'How kind of you to let me experience this.' But you can say, 'How awesome and beautiful you must be to have made something this exquisite'."

As you do that, pondering God's works leads to prayers of adoration.

Your very personal God

God is not the un-knowable God of Spinoza and Einstein, a God who orders and creates but remains impersonal, distant and uncaring. He has drawn near to us in Jesus. He has drawn us to himself tenderly, with fatherly affection.

"When I look at your heavens, the work of your fingers, the moon and the stars, which you have set in place, what is man that you are mindful of him, and the son of man that you care for him? Yet you have made him a little lower than the heavenly beings and crowned him with glory and honor. You have given him dominion over the works of your hands; you have put all things under his feet, all sheep and oxen, and also the beasts of the field, the birds of the heavens, and the fish of the sea, whatever passes along the paths of the seas. O LORD, our Lord, how majestic is your name in all the earth!" (Psalm 8)

Contemplating the majesty of God's world is like priming the pump. It gets you thinking about the greatness of God.

Ponder also the way God has provided for you and sustained your life. How has he worked in your life to bring you to the place where you are now? How have you seen his goodness in providence?

And ponder the glory of God in Jesus Christ. Think deeply about Jesus humbling himself, setting aside his rights as Lord and King and Creator to take on humanity – to become one of us in order to save. Think of this infinite God being willing to suffer in order to rescue creatures. Think of God's redeeming love for you in Christ.

Then tell him what you think: "If what you made is this beautiful, how much more beautiful must you be? If you're able to sustain all these ecosystems, to provide for the fish, the birds, the animals, forgive me for doubting your ability to take care of me. Forgive me for being filled with so much worry or with anger about the way I think (wrongly) you're not taking care of me."

PART III

"Your kingdom come, your will be done on earth as it is in heaven."

OUR CULTURE TEACHES US to be focused on ourselves. It is easy to think about what I want, what would make me happy, and what I think should be done in any given situation. I tend to carry that way of thinking into my relationship with God and into my prayer life. I can easily think God exists to help me accomplish my goals. I know I'm thinking like that when I feel disappointed or frustrated about something. Disappointment reveals expectations that haven't been met. I stop and consider what I wanted to see happen that didn't happen. And I begin to see that I expected God to help me write with the script I have written for my own life.

God is writing a story of redemption, and it's a far bigger story than I understand. And when God rescued me from the dominion of darkness and brought me into the Kingdom of his Son, he put me into his story. Instead of asking God to endorse my views of what life should be all about, the Bible calls me to something much greater. It's not my will and what I want that is most important. What God wants –his will– is what matters most. What God wants is ultimately what is best.

Jesus taught us to pray that God's will would be done on earth in the same way it is done in heaven. I can't imagine angels in heaven questioning God's goodness or wisdom when he gives them a command. Only fallen people do that. What if we delighted in doing what God commanded and found joy in pursuing God's will like the angels in heaven? What if our greatest desire would be for the advancement of God's kingdom in our world, rather than the advancement of our little kingdoms?

How do we develop a desire for God's will and God's kingdom purposes in the world? The psalms give us models for prayer that will help us understand what it means to pray, *"Your kingdom come, your will be done on earth as it is in heaven."*

Chapter 7

Thirsty for God

ON THE NIGHT HE WAS BETRAYED, Jesus instituted what we call the Lord's Supper. In abstract theological language he could have said, "I am about to become the propitiation for sin. It is only through substitutionary atonement that God can be just and the one who justifies the guilty."

That would have been true, but his disciples would have been left scratching their heads. Jesus understood the power of metaphor. He used figures of speech that made ideas more vivid and alive to people's minds and hearts. Jesus didn't use abstract ideas to communicate the truth we need to hear. He used imagery that we understand.

He said: *"I am the vine. If you abide in me, you will bear much fruit."* His followers saw grape vines all the time. A cluster of grapes can't live disconnected from the vine. It has no life in itself. The grapes will dry up and blow away if they are cut off from the vine. The point is clear: staying connected to Christ is vital for us.

Jesus said, *"I am the good shepherd." "I am the light of the world." "I am the bread of life."* When you read all these metaphors, you might ask, "Which one are you, Jesus? Are you the vine, the shepherd, the light, or the bread?" But all of those metaphors help us to grasp the truth about who Jesus is and what it means to be united to him by faith.

Think a bit more about Jesus as the bread. In John 6, the Apostle John told the story of Jesus feeding five thousand people from a boy's lunch of five loaves of bread and two small fish. People were hungry. There was nowhere nearby that Jesus could send them to buy food for themselves. So he miraculously multiplied that boy's lunch and fed a huge crowd. There were about five thousand men, in addition to women and children – that's a lot of people to feed! When they had all eaten their fill, the people were amazed. They were ready to make Jesus king by force. So he quietly slipped away from them. But the next day, they came looking for him. They were hungry again, and a man who could feed them miraculously would be a great king!

When they found Jesus, he said to them:

"Truly, truly, I say to you, you are seeking me, not because you saw signs, but because you ate your fill of the loaves. Do not labor for the food that perishes, but for the food that endures to eternal life, which the Son of Man will give to you."

"Then they said to him, 'What must we do, to be doing the works of God?' Jesus answered them, 'This is the work of God, that you believe in him whom he has sent.'

"They responded by asking Jesus what sign he would give them so they could believe him. They said, 'Our fathers ate manna in the wilderness; as it is written, 'He gave them bread from heaven to eat'. Jesus said to them, 'Truly, truly I say to you, it was not Moses who gave you the bread from heaven, but my Father who gives you the true bread from heaven. For the bread of God is he who comes down from heaven and gives life to the world.'

"They said, 'Sir, give us this bread always.'

"Jesus said to them, 'I am the bread of life, whoever comes to me shall not go hungry and whoever believes in me shall never thirst'" (John 6:26-35).

They didn't understand what he was talking about because they didn't understand who he was. They were looking for another Moses who could give them what the people received after the Exodus from Egypt – food they didn't have to work for! Jesus was offering them something much better. It was food they wouldn't have to work for, but food that would satisfy a deeper hunger.

Their forefathers had been fed in the desert by God, who provided a kind of bread for the people every morning – manna! Bread, even supernaturally provided bread, satisfies hunger for a while. But people need something more than physical bread. There is a hunger in our souls that nothing in this world can satisfy!

On another occasion, Jesus said, "If anyone thirsts, let him come to me and drink. Whoever believes in me, as the Scripture has said, 'Out of his heart will flow rivers of living water'" (John 7:37b-38).

Do you understand what Jesus was talking about? Do you know what it means to be hungry or thirsty for something that can't be satisfied by anything this world can give you?

What are you hungry for?

When Jesus says *"If anyone thirsts, let him come to me and drink"*, it sounds like he's inviting people who don't yet know him as Savior and Lord to come to faith. It is true that sinful people are hungry and thirsty and that they try to satisfy their longings in sinful ways:

Some people are hungry for power – they have to be in control.

Greed is a kind of hunger or thirst. Greed says, "I will really be happy if I just have a little more than I have now." Anger often reveals a deep hunger – a demand to have things my way! Lust is a kind of hunger. Men and women do all kinds of destructive things to find satisfaction for that hunger.

But it's not just unsaved, lost people who are hungry and thirsty. If you pass off what the Bible says about being hungry and thirsty to people who are chasing after sex or drugs or alcohol or gluttony, you will end up missing something that you need to see about yourself! We are all hungry, thirsty people, trying to find satisfaction for our hunger and thirst in things that will not ultimately satisfy! Sin distorts our longings and the ways we seek satisfaction, but the things we hunger and thirst after are not necessarily sinful in themselves. We're hungry for good things, legitimate pleasures, things God created and meant for us to enjoy:

We long for these good things:
- To be loved and valued by your parents.
- To be happily married to a man or woman who cares about you deeply.
- To enjoy good food.
- To have children who love you and want to be around you!
- To be able to get up day after day and actually enjoy going to work because it is exactly what you always wanted to do with your life.
- To be able to earn enough money to not have to worry about how you are going to pay the bills.
- To know that your life matters – that it makes a difference to someone that you have lived.
- To know you have used your gifts and abilities in a way that honors God.
- To be respected by people whose opinion matters to you.

These desires at times feel as strong as hunger or thirst. Sometimes these desires are actually stronger than your desire to eat! We spend our energy; we devote our strength and abilities to satisfying those hungers and thirsts. When you are thirsty, you can't just ignore your thirst!

When Jesus used the language of hunger and thirst, he used words that should have been familiar to people who knew the Scriptures:

"Come, everyone who thirsts, come to the waters; and he who has no money, come, buy and eat! Come, buy wine and milk without money and without price. Why do you spend your money for that which is not bread, and your labor for that which does not satisfy? Listen diligently to me, and eat what is good, and delight yourselves in rich food. Incline your ear, and come to me; hear, that your soul may live…" (Isaiah 55:1-2).

We are hungry people. We are thirsty people. We think if we can earn enough, we can buy what we need to satisfy our hunger and thirst. But we end up spending our money on things that don't satisfy. We spend our hard work on things that don't last. God comes and says, "Come to me, and I will give you food and drink that really satisfies. I will fill that hunger and satisfy that thirst in your soul. Come to me and find life!" And Jesus offered exactly the same thing. He offered himself as the one who can satisfy what our souls long for most deeply.

What do you desire?

If you are honest, what do you want more than anything? You know you're supposed to say at this point, "I desire God more than anything!" But what do your disappointments suggest you are hungry for? What do your choices this past week suggest you are thirsting for?

God said to Israel: *"My people have committed two evils: they have forsaken me, the spring of living water, and have dug their own cisterns, broken cisterns that can hold no water"* (Jeremiah 2:13).

He is not just describing people who have never come to faith in Christ. He's describing us! This is what sinners do – even redeemed sinners! God offers himself as a pure, refreshing spring of water that gives life. We turn away and dig our own wells in an attempt to satisfy our thirsts without God. It usually takes a while, but sooner or later we discover that the wells we dig for ourselves can't hold water. We take good things and elevate them to the place of ultimate things. We take legitimate, good desires like having children, being married, being financially secure, and being respected and make them the most important things in life.

Sooner or later we start to feel like something is still missing. When good things are elevated to the level of best things, they become idols – substitute gods. And false gods can't meet real needs! It is one thing to be told that the wells we dig for ourselves won't satisfy. It's another thing to experience that emptiness for ourselves. We agree intellectually with God's assessment of our problem but that doesn't mean we quit digging those wells. A fresh experience of disappointment is all it takes to expose the well digging in our hearts.

And it's not like you figure this out at one point in your life and quit digging your own wells! Even as redeemed people this is our default tendency – this is what we do! We keep on digging our own wells to try to satisfy a thirst we feel inside rather than drinking from the spring of living water that God offers in himself.

"Jesus, thou joy of loving hearts, Thou fount of life, Thou light of men, from the best bliss that earth imparts, we turn unfilled to Thee again" (Bernard of Clairvaux).

The hymn writer did not deny the goodness of the things we pursue in this world. God has given us good things to enjoy. But even the "best bliss that earth imparts" leaves us unfilled. You have experienced that in one way or another. We all have some level of experience with the "best bliss that earth imparts" – tasty food, cold water on a hot day, good friendships, beautiful music, amazing sights. We experience moments of bliss, moments of satisfaction for legitimate longings. But those moments don't last. The bliss fades. A longing deep inside is left unsatisfied. But we don't instinctively do what Bernard of Clairvaux said: "we turn unfilled to Thee again."

Instead, *we turn unfilled* to another attempt to satisfy our hunger and thirst by digging a new well to drink from.

We are all hungry, thirsty people who look to something other than God to satisfy our longings.

You know that's true. You can affirm what I'm saying and nod your head in agreement, but *how do we get our hearts to long for God Himself more than we long for other things?*

A heart problem

What God said to Israel and what Jesus said to hungry and thirsty people is that he alone can satisfy our deepest hunger and thirst. We know that in our heads. It's our hearts that deceive us over and over again.

Jesus said, *"Do not lay up for yourselves treasures on earth, where moth and rust destroy and where thieves break in and steal, but lay up for yourselves treasures in heaven, where neither moth nor rust destroys and where thieves do not break in and steal. For where your treasure is, there your heart will be also"* (Matthew 6:19-21).

What you want most is what you treasure. Your heart will follow or chase after what you value most. If your heart values things that can be stolen or destroyed by rust or moths, you will be disappointed sooner or later. There's only one safe place to lay up treasure – in heaven. And there is only one treasure that will truly and eternally satisfy your heart – God himself.

So how do you get your heart to that place? How do you change what you desire and long for?

Just telling yourself that you should desire something different won't change your longings! You can't change your heart by trying harder to long for God. Will power, making resolutions, and trying harder to discipline yourself will not change your heart's desires.

But God can do what you are powerless to do! God can change the desires of your heart. The way God changes our desires is by the work of the Holy Spirit who quietly and gradually enables us to see Jesus as more desirable and beautiful than anything else. As God's Spirit draws you and stirs your heart with longing for God, you begin to see the glory of Jesus in ways you did not see before.

Wouldn't you love to be able to say what the psalmists say, and mean it:

*"O God, you are my God; earnestly I seek you; **my soul thirsts for you**; my flesh faints for you, as in a dry and weary land where there is no water. So I have looked upon you in the sanctuary, beholding your power and glory. Because your steadfast love is better than life, my lips will praise you"* (Psalm 63:1-3).

*"As a deer pants for flowing streams, so pants my soul for you, O God. **My soul thirsts for God, for the living God"*** (Psalm 42:1-2).

"Whom have I in heaven but you? **And there is nothing on earth that I desire besides you.** *My flesh and my heart may fail, but God is the strength of my heart, and my portion forever"* (Psalm 73:25-26).

"Preserve me, O God, for in you I take refuge. I say to the LORD, 'You are my Lord; **I have no good apart from you.** *The LORD is my chosen portion and my cup. You make known to me the path of life; in your presence there is fullness of joy; at your right hand are pleasures forevermore'"* (Psalm 16:1-2,11).

You can't make yourself thirsty for God. But you can ask God to change your heart and give you new longings. What about asking God to make you thirsty for him? You could pray something like this:

"Father, show me where I tend to turn away from you and dig my own wells. Let me see the truth about where I am trying to satisfy the thirst of my heart apart from you. Show me your beauty and glory. Show me the richness of your love. Show me how you are more to be desired than any of the things in life I look to for happiness. Make me thirsty for you."

To have a deep hunger and thirst for God, you need to grow in understanding who he is. God's Spirit shows you the beauty and glory of Jesus through the Scriptures. Ask God, as you read a section of Scripture, to show you something more of his majesty and glory and beauty.

"When [David] proclaimed, 'Your love is better than life,' he wasn't saying 'Your love makes life worth living' or 'With your love I can do anything;' rather, he was saying, 'I love being loved by you more than I love being alive.' How does one's heart come alive to this kind of relationship with God?

"...David wrote these words from a hot Judean desert at a time of great internal conflict and weariness. Among other heartaches, his own son Absalom sought to take David's life. Difficult circumstances and hard providences often become a primary means by which the Holy Spirit quickens our thirst for the fountain that God alone can open up. No one and nothing but God can satisfy the cravings he has placed within the hearts of his children. We are our most sane and free when we live in light of this truth.

"Spurgeon spoke well when he said, 'This is an insatiable longing after one of the essentials of life. There is no reasoning with this longing, no forgetting it, no despising it, no overcoming it by stoical indifference. Thirst will be heard. The whole person must yield to its power. So it is with the divine power that the grace of God creates. It is a gift to be thirsty for God'" (Scotty Smith, *Objects of His Affection*, p. 85-86).

Fight for joy

If God is the one who creates this kind of thirst for himself in your heart as a work of grace, asking him for that gift must become a regular part of our petitions in prayer. We need to ask God to do in our hearts what we are incapable of doing. And we need to plead with God to do this work of grace in our hearts daily!

When you hear John Piper preach or read one of his books, his passion for God is striking. So it's a bit surprising to hear Dr. Piper say that he has to fight for joy every day. Here's what he said about his struggle and about how he prays for God to work in his heart:

"Almost every day I pray early in the morning that God would give me desires for him and his Word, because the desires I ought to have are absent or weak…Here is the way I pray:

"INCLINE: The first thing my soul needs is an inclination toward God and his Word. Without that, nothing else will happen of any value in my life. I must want to know God and read his Word and draw near to him. So Psalm 119:36 teaches us to pray, *'Incline my heart to your testimonies, and not to selfish gain.'* Very simply we ask God to take our hearts, which are more inclined to breakfast and the newspaper, and change that inclination. We are asking God to create desires that are not there.

"OPEN: Next I need to have the eyes of my heart opened so that when my inclination leads me to the Word, I see what is really there, and not just my own ideas. Who opens the eyes of the heart? God does. So Psalm 119:18 teaches us to pray, *'Open my eyes, that I may behold wondrous things out of your law.'* So many times we read the Bible and see nothing wonderful. Its reading does not produce joy. So what can we do? We can cry to God, 'Open the eyes of my heart, O Lord, to see what it says about you as wonderful.'

"UNITE: Then I am concerned that my heart is badly fragmented. Parts of it are inclined, and parts of it are not. Parts see wonder, and parts say, 'That's not so wonderful.' What I long for is a united heart where all the parts say a joyful **Yes!** to what God reveals in his Word. Where does that wholeness and unity come from? It comes from God. So Psalm 86:11 teaches us to pray, *'Unite my heart to fear your name.'* Don't stumble over the word fear when you thought we were seeking joy. The fear of the Lord is a joyful experience when you renounce all sin. A thunderstorm can be a trembling joy when you know you can't be destroyed by lightning. *'O Lord, let your ear be attentive to…the prayer of your servants who delight to fear your name'* (Nehemiah 1:11). *'His delight shall be in the fear of the LORD'* (Isaiah 11:3). Therefore pray that God would unite your heart to joyfully fear the Lord.

"SATISFY: What I really want from all this engagement with the Word of God and the work of the Spirit in answer to my prayers is for my heart to be satisfied with God and not with the world. Where does that satisfaction come from? It comes from God. So Psalm 90:14 teaches us to pray, *'Satisfy us in the morning with your steadfast love, that we may rejoice and be glad all our days.'*

"…for my part, the only hope I have to love God as I ought is that he would overcome all my disinclination and bind my heart to himself in love. That is the grace I must have to be a Christian and to live in joy.

"So… 'I pray to God repeatedly: Incline my heart! Open the eyes of my heart! Unite my heart! Satisfy my heart!' Prayer is, therefore, not only the measure of our hearts, revealing what we really desire; it is also the indispensible remedy for our hearts when we do not desire God the way we ought" (John Piper, *When I Don't Desire God*, pages 150-153).

I encourage you to ask God to make you thirsty for himself, not just for any good gifts he might give you. Ask him to work in your heart so you will long for him. Ask him to open his Word to you so you will know him. And ask him to show you in your experience his goodness and beauty and wisdom and desirability.

"It is a gift to be thirsty for God!"

Chapter 8

Declare His Glory Among the Nations

MY WIFE AND I HAD A NINE-HOUR DELAY in the Newark Airport a few months ago on our way back from a conference in Spain. Our connecting flight to Orlando was canceled because of some bad weather, so we spent a long time waiting. And as we waited, I watched the people.

There were hundreds and hundreds of people moving through the halls of just that one part of the airport. There were people of all kinds of shapes and sizes and colors and nationalities. I saw a Coptic monk, a few Hasidic Jews, people from India, Japan, China, the Middle East, and the Philippines. There were overweight people, skinny people, tattooed people, old people, young people. There were happy people and angry people, no doubt angry about canceled flights! So many, many people – all going somewhere as fast as they could walk.

It reminded me of an ant farm. Maybe you've seen those glass-sided thin boxes of sand full of ants. The ants make tunnels along the glass and all the ants on one side of the box decide they have to be on the other side, so back and forth they go as fast as they can.

I wondered, "Is this what it's like for God to watch people?" Then I thought, "How can God possibly know all these people?" And there are millions more crawling around in places other than airports all around the world right now. Do we look like ants racing back and forth in an ant farm to God?

How many people do you know? That probably depends on how you define the word "know". If "know" means that I've seen them somewhere before, I know a lot of people. I recognize their faces. I've seen them in a store somewhere or on the street. But I don't know all their names.

The circle of people you know by name is smaller: friends, family members, people you work with. You know more about them. You've shared experiences with them.

But how many people do you really know well? For how many can you describe what they want most in life or what stirs their hearts? How many of them do you know well enough to know how they'll respond in a given situation or what they are afraid of or what has grieved them? In this category, there are probably very few you really "know."

Because we can only know and care for a limited number of people, we can't imagine God knowing and caring for an unlimited number of people. But God's capacity for relationships is infinite – it has no limitations of time, distance or knowledge. He doesn't depend on what people tell him about themselves for what he knows about them. He knows everything about every single human being who has lived or ever will live.

The Psalmist said, *"O LORD, you have searched me and know me"* (Psalm 139). He knows your thoughts – even before you think them. And the psalmist says that kind of knowledge is *"too wonderful for me, it is high, I cannot attain it."* That God knows me better than I know myself is an amazing thought. But to realize that God knows every human being with that kind of complete knowledge is beyond me – I can't begin to comprehend that kind of knowledge!

Maybe the bigger questions are: "Why would God want to know all those people? And why would God care about all of them?" But then again, maybe those questions reveal more about me than they reveal about God. Honestly, I don't want to know all those people I see in the airport. I don't care about them. And since I don't care about them, I think, why would God?

God desires relationships

The good news is that God is not like me! For that matter, he's not like you, either!

"When I look at your heavens, the work of your fingers, the moon and the stars, which you have set in place, what is man that you are mindful of him, and the son of man that you care for him?" (Psalm 8:3-4)

It's an amazing thing that the God who created the vastness of space with its billions of stars and planets, would care about human beings on this small planet. It's not just that God cares about human beings in general. God's desire for relationship is vast, and his capacity for relationships is infinite! He actually wants to know a vast number of people.

And God invites us to join in his passion for gathering a people from the nations of this world for his own possession, for his everlasting glory.

Psalm 96:1-3: *"Oh sing to the LORD a new song; sing to the LORD, all the earth! Sing to the LORD, bless his name; tell of his salvation from day to day. Declare his glory among the nations, his marvelous works among all the peoples!"*

The command is to proclaim, to declare the glory and greatness of God among all the nations. But it starts with a command to sing! You can't invite people to sing to the LORD if you are not singing, that is, if you are not excited and moved by who God is and what he has done.

"Declare his glory among the nations, his marvelous works among all the peoples! For great is the LORD, and greatly to be praised; he is to be feared above all gods. For all the gods of the peoples are worthless idols, but the LORD made the heavens. Splendor and majesty are before him; strength and beauty are in his sanctuary" (Psalm 96:3-6).

God calls us to proclaim the truth. Tell the nations and peoples of the earth the truth about who God is. Show them his surpassing greatness. The things they are trusting are empty and worthless, but power and beauty belong to God. The gods people worship and trust are powerless to do anything in their lives. They will not save them. They are unable to help them. There is no beauty in false gods.

We are to tell people about the marvelous things God has done not only in creation and providence, but in the work of redemption. This is not a boring message. It's not just religious information! We are to declare the majesty and glory of God and to tell about his marvelous works!

And we are to invite them to join in the praise of God

"Ascribe to the LORD, O families of the peoples, ascribe to the LORD glory and strength! Ascribe to the LORD the glory due his name; bring an offering and come into his courts! Worship the LORD in the splendor of holiness; tremble before him, all the earth! Say among the nations, "The LORD reigns!" (Psalm 96:7-10).

We are also to warn the nations of coming judgment:

"Yes, the world is established; it shall never be moved; he will judge the peoples with equity." Let the heavens be glad, and let the earth rejoice; let the sea roar, and all that fills it; let the field exult, and everything in it! Then shall all the trees of the forest sing for joy before the LORD, for he comes, for he comes to judge the earth. He will judge the world in righteousness, and the peoples in his faithfulness" (Psalm 96:10-13).

God claims the allegiance of all people, in every imaginable culture and place. Every human being will stand before God in the end, so how they respond to God now matters eternally!

As you read the Psalms, looking for what you can learn about prayer, it's easy to focus on things like:

Giving thanks.

Confessing your sin to God, coming in honest repentance.

Expressing your needs and asking for wisdom. You can tell God what is confusing to you about the way he works in your life.

Delighting your soul in God, meditating on his words and works…

God's heart for nations

There is a lot you can find in the psalms about how you should relate to God. But the psalms also show us what God cares about and invite us to share a passion for what is on God's heart!

This is what God reveals about himself: he is not a kind of tribal deity, just the God of Abraham and his descendants, content to have one people group that belongs to him. God's heart for the families and tribes and nations and peoples of this world is clear all through the Bible!

When he called Abraham to faith and entered into a covenant with Abraham, one of the promises God gave to Abraham was: "…in you all the families of the earth shall be blessed" (Genesis 12:3b).

Psalm 2 is a messianic psalm that also affirms God's heart for the nations:

"You are my Son; today I have begotten you….Ask of me, and I will make the nations your heritage, and the ends of the earth your possession. You shall break them with a rod of iron and dash them in pieces like a potter's vessel. Now therefore, O kings, be wise; be warned, O rulers of the earth. Serve the LORD with fear, and rejoice with trembling. Kiss the Son, lest he be angry, and you perish in the way, for his wrath is quickly kindled. Blessed are all who take refuge in him."

"All" who take refuge in him means who? All the Jewish people through the centuries who heard these words read in the Temple or the synagogue? No, all from the nations of the world who take refuge in him; all who "kiss the Son" by submitting to him, honoring him as LORD; all who find God to be their Refuge!

God's heart for the nations that is declared so often in the psalms echoes through the pages of the whole Bible.

Isaiah tells us what is on the heart of the coming Messiah, the Servant of the LORD:

"…and now the LORD says – he who formed me in the womb to be his servant to bring Jacob back to him and gather Israel to himself, for I am honored in the eyes of the LORD and my God has been my strength – he says, "It is too small a thing for you to be my servant to restore the tribes of Jacob and bring back those of Israel I have kept. I will also make you a light for the Gentiles, that you may bring my salvation to the ends of the earth" (Isaiah 49:5-6).

"…On this mountain the LORD of hosts will make for all peoples a feast of rich food, a feast of well-aged wine, of rich food full of marrow, of aged wine well refined. And he will swallow up on this mountain the covering that is cast over all peoples, the veil that is spread over all nations. He will swallow up death forever; and the LORD God will wipe away tears from all faces. It will be said on that day, 'Behold, this is our God; we have waited for him, that he might save us. This is the LORD; we have waited for him; let us be glad and rejoice in his salvation'" (Isaiah 25:6-9).

Several centuries later, the apostle Paul explained to the people of Athens:

The God who made the world and everything in it, being Lord of heaven and earth, does not live in temples made by man, nor is he served by human hands, as though he needed anything, since he himself gives to all mankind life and breath and everything. And he made from one man every nation of mankind to live on all the face of the earth, having determined allotted periods and the boundaries of their dwelling place, that they should SEEK GOD, in the hope that they might feel their way toward him and find him. Yet he is actually not far from each one of us… (Acts 17:24-27).

Nations and people groups are divided by cultural differences and language barriers. There was a time when everyone spoke a common language. Genesis 11 tells the story of God scattering the people around the world and confusing their languages. So God created all the diversity of language and race and culture that we find around the world. God determined when individual people would live and where they would live. Ethnic differences are something God created, Paul tells the people of Athens, with a desire that people would seek him and find him.

It was not that some people might seek for God eventually and maybe they would find him. God's intention has always been to gather a people for himself from all these races and tribes and language groups. God longs to see people come to repentance!

"The Lord is not slow to fulfill his promise as some count slowness, but is patient toward you, not wishing that any should perish but that all should reach repentance" (II Peter 3:9).

God's incredible patience

Peter actually tells us in that passage that God patiently delays the return of Jesus because God is unwilling to let people perish. He intends to save more before the final day!

When Peter says, *"he is not willing that any should perish but that all should come to repentance,"* what does he mean by "willing?" The Bible talks about the sovereign will of God by which God accomplishes whatever he determines to accomplish. Whatever God "wills" in this sense comes to pass. But that can't be what Peter means in II Peter 3, or he would be saying God is sovereignly determining that everyone will be saved. That's not what the rest of Scripture teaches.

So the English Standard Version, for example, has tried to capture the meaning by saying *"not wishing"* that any should perish. That means God takes no delight in people being lost, he longs for all kinds of people to come to repentance.

As you try to reconcile the sovereignty of God in salvation and the free will of people in choosing whether or not to trust in Christ, don't downplay the vastness of the missionary heart of God that is expressed in that sentence! God actually desires a vast number of people to be saved from all the tribes and language groups and people groups and nations of this world! And that's why he has delayed the return of

Jesus and the Day of Judgment.

Psalm 96: *"Oh sing to the LORD a new song; sing to the LORD, all the earth! Sing to the LORD, bless his name; tell of his salvation from day to day. Declare his glory among the nations, his marvelous works among all the peoples!"*

When the psalmist calls us to declare God's glory among the nations, he is calling us to share in God's passion for missions. Part of our joy as redeemed and loved people, who know the grace and mercy of God in Christ Jesus is to see people from other nations and people groups come to salvation.

Passion for people

My wife, Margaret, and I had the opportunity to spend a week in Spain with the World Harvest Mission family where she serves on the board of directors. Every three years they gather all their missionaries from all the various places where they are serving for a week of reflection, restoration, encouragement, training and fellowship.

World Harvest Mission is a small mission organization (they have around one hundred and seventy missionaries) and this is just one mission organization among many from North America. There were about four hundred people there as part of the conference, and I was glad for nametags.

At dinner the first night, I said to Margaret (who is the definition of an extrovert), "This is an extrovert's dream and an introvert's nightmare!" I am an introvert. I could see it in her eyes – she felt compelled to meet every one of those four hundred people. I, on the other hand, thought, "I really don't want to meet any of these people." (Remember, I'm the one in the airport who didn't want to know any of those people or care about them, either.)

I did pretty well for an introvert! I met a lot of people and heard a lot of great stories about what God was doing in people's lives. It was not just fun, it was very moving!

Some of those missionaries have served with World Harvest Mission for thirty years (from the time Jack Miller went to Uganda and started the mission organization). But most of the missionaries were young – in their twenties and thirties. There was a group of five or six doctors and their families who have moved to Burundi to serve in a hospital. The team leader is in his fifties, but all the rest of the doctors are young. There was a group of men who could make a good living in the United States who have chosen to raise support, go to language school for a year to learn French, and move their families to the middle of Africa to serve a poor community in the name of Christ!

I listened one afternoon to the report from a group of young singles and couples who have chosen to go to Islamic countries as doctors, dentists, and artists. They have moved their families into areas that are highly resistant to the gospel. Having spent a week in Cairo, Egypt a couple of years ago, I can't imagine choosing to live in that kind of culture.

I had lunch one day with a clinical psychologist and his wife, a man who has taught on the university level, who is now raising support to go to Vienna (very appropriate for a psychologist – that's where Freud was from). They told me the reason they wanted to move to Vienna is that less than one percent of the population in Vienna is Christian.

I met a young couple who recently moved to a remote town near the Himalayan border in India. They talked about large numbers of people who are asking about Christianity. They are seeing a tremendous hunger for the gospel.

But I thought many times during those days, "What compels young people to give up the American dream to give their lives to missions?" I think it's a conviction that what Psalm 96:5 says is absolutely true:

"For all the gods of the peoples are worthless idols, but the LORD made the heavens. Splendor and majesty are before him; strength and beauty are in his sanctuary."

The reason people are willing to give up a comfortable life in a culture that has abundance are convictions like these:

People are lost and without hope apart from Christ.

As God's Word is proclaimed, he will draw people to faith.

God really does intend to gather people from all the nations and peoples.

God calls his people to declare his glory among the nations.

"Declare his glory among the nations, his marvelous works among all the peoples!" (Psalm 96:3)

Declare his glory

"Declare his glory" is another way of describing the task of proclamation. How will anyone hear the gospel of God's grace in Jesus Christ unless someone tells them? And how can anyone tell them unless some are sent with the message? God's people are sent by God to the nations, to all the peoples of the world with the message of God's saving grace in Jesus Christ.

How will we do that? How will we, in our church families, declare his glory among the nations, his marvelous works among all the peoples?

Through the years God has raised up people from our church family who felt God was calling them to go to another people group in a distant nation to declare God's glory:

Craig and Debbie Rice left a dental practice to serve in New Guinea.

Joe and Elise Armfield went with Wycliffe.

James and Joyce Repp went to Japan.

Carolyn and RJ March went to London.

Brett and Taylor Rayl went to Japan.

Jamie Amick went to Ireland.

John and Cathy Drobnick took an early retirement to serve with New Tribes Mission.

Many others have gone on short term mission trips.

Some of us will be called by God to go to another nation or people group, to learn a new language, to become part of a different culture in order to declare God's glory to people who haven't heard about Jesus. But most of us will assist in declaring God's glory to the nations by giving in order to send those God calls to go.

Going and Sending

In terms of the command – *"Declare his glory among the nations, his marvelous works among all the peoples"* – some will be called to go. Most of us will be part of sending. But is that it? Let me suggest a couple more things. Missions isn't just about what happens in other places. God is bringing the nations to us!

In our community, hundreds of Chinese students come to the University of Central Florida every year! At nearby Port Canaveral there is a ministry to people from all over the world who work on freighters and cruise ships who can't get off those ships because they don't have passports or visas. In our small town we have people from South and Central America, India, Brazil, the Middle East, and many more places. And there are lots of plain old Americans who are not yet singing God's praises because their hearts are given to false gods.

You can have a part in reaching people with the gospel of God's grace by befriending people. And you can pray about God's glory among the nations. Maybe you are good about praying for missions and about interceding for missionaries you help support. But most of us, when we think, "What should I pray for?" don't often think about missions or God's passion for the nations. I want to urge you to learn from the psalms to pray for the nations, for the peoples, and for God's glory among the nations.

God ordains the end – the salvation of a vast number of people from every tribe, language, people, and nation – and God ordains the means for this saving work by providing someone to tell them about Christ. God saves people through the proclamation of the gospel as people are sent with the message. And God ordains to do all this through the prayers of his people.

John Piper in his excellent book on missions, *"Let the Nations Be Glad"* says this: "...Not only has God made the accomplishment of his purposes hang on the preaching of the word; he has also made the success of that preaching hang on prayer. God's goal to be glorified will not succeed without the powerful proclamation of the gospel. And that gospel will not be proclaimed in power to all the nations without the prevailing, earnest, faith-filled prayers of God's people."

Many years ago, a man named A.T. Pierson said:

"Every new Pentecost has had its preparatory period of supplication…God has compelled his saints to seek Him at the throne of grace, so that every new advance might be so plainly due to His power that even the unbeliever might be constrained to confess: 'Surely this is the finger of God'."

And again, John Piper:

"When missions moves forward by prayer it magnifies the power of God. When it moves forward by human management it magnifies man."

I urge you to pray for missionaries. Ask God to place them on your heart and remind you to pray. Pray what? In general, you can pray these kinds of things as you think about missions and missionaries:

- For an outpouring of the Holy Spirit on that city, that culture, that nation, an outpouring like Pentecost.

- For encouragement in the gospel for that missionary family.

- For boldness (that's what Paul asked people to pray for on his behalf).

- For protection, especially for those serving in places that are hostile to Christianity.

- For a growing heart for God's glory as the driving motivation for mission.

- For daily bread.

- For rest and restoration.

- For a supernatural ability to love the unlovely.

Pray for your church

Ask God to give you eyes to see the peoples he has brought to your church! Ask God for opportunities to make friends with people from different ethnic backgrounds. Pray for an outpouring of the Holy Spirit on your hometown. Pray for boldness for your church family in declaring the gospel. Pray for a heart for God's glory. Ask God to give you eyes to see people as God sees them – harassed and helpless, like sheep without a shepherd. Ask for an ability to love the unlovely. Ask God to do what you are powerless to do. You can't convince people to believe the gospel, but you can pray and ask God to bring them to faith through the proclamation of His Word.

"When I look at your heavens, the work of your fingers, the moon and the stars, which you have set in place, what is man that you are mindful of him, and the son of man that you care for him?" (Psalm 8:3-4)

I can't explain why God cares about people the way he does. It's an amazing thing that the God who created the vastness of space with its billions of stars and planets, would care about human beings on this small planet. But he does. And he invites us to share in his passion for gathering a people for his glory from all the nations.

PART IV

"Give us today our daily bread..."

HEN MOST PEOPLE ASK YOU TO PRAY ABOUT SOMETHING, they are asking you to petition God, to ask God, on their behalf. Prayer is more than setting petitions before God, but it involves asking. God invites us to come to him and ask. By asking we recognize our complete dependence on God for everything.

As we ask God for things that matter to us, we should also thank him for what he has done.

Chapter 9

Can You Say Thank You?

"*W*HAT HAS GOD EVER DONE FOR ME?" The question was asked in all seriousness, but I couldn't believe what I was hearing.

Most people in the world today and most people who have ever lived on this planet would consider the young man who asked the question highly privileged. He grew up with parents who loved him and gave him all kinds of opportunities to learn and explore life. He had been healthy and strong all his life. He was intelligent and well educated, having attended some of the best of schools up through college. He had traveled around the world and seen things most people will never have the opportunity to see. And he grew up attending church with his family and hearing the Bible read and taught by his parents, by pastors, and by gifted Bible teachers.

But somewhere along the line he decided he could no longer believe what the Bible said. He doesn't claim to be an atheist. He doesn't deny that there may be a God out there somewhere. But if there is a God, he surmised he was not involved in our lives in any meaningful or practical way. After all, as he said, "What has God ever done for me?"

Part of his disillusionment stems from his experience with prayer. He had prayed and asked God to intervene in certain situations, but what he asked God to do didn't happen. He can't see the kindness and goodness of God in all the things God has done for him because he is focused on disappointment over what God hasn't done for him.

It still hasn't occurred to him that the problem might not be God's existence or God's goodness but his view of God. The reality is, his disappointment with God is tied to a shallow concept of God.

A God who is little more than a heavenly Santa Claus who exists to respond to our wish lists won't make sense when you experience heartbreaking disappointments or in the face of destructive things like marriage breakdowns, violent cruelty, cancer, famine, and war.

When people ask this Celestial Santa Claus to help them or to provide something they want, and it doesn't happen, they get angry and resentful toward God and toward Christians who believe what the Bible says about God.

How can you thank a God who doesn't do what you think he should do? How can you be thankful if you don't get what you want in life?

An irrelevant God?

That young man is not alone in his ingratitude. A lack of gratitude toward God is characteristic of the whole human race. It's one of the marks of our fallen, sinful condition. C.S. Lewis defined human beings as "The Ungrateful Bipeds."

Ingratitude is characteristic of unbelief:

*"For what can be known about God is plain to them, because God has shown it to them. For his invisible attributes, namely, his eternal power and divine nature, have been clearly perceived, ever since the creation of the world, in the things that have been made. So they are without excuse. For although they knew God, they did not honor him as God **or give thanks to him**, but they became futile in their thinking, and their foolish hearts were darkened..."* (Romans 1:19-21).

Paul is not suggesting that all these people have become atheists. Most people in the ancient world believed there were gods out there. But God was irrelevant to them. They chose to chase after something else, to satisfy the desires in their hearts with something other than God.

That's true of most people in our culture. Not many actually claim to be atheists. They won't deny that God might be out there somewhere. But he's irrelevant to daily life. If God is there at all, he means well, but he can't protect anyone from bad things that happen.

Even in churches you hear this idea of God. I was at a funeral a few years ago of a friend who was killed in a car accident. The pastor stood up and said, "God didn't mean for this to happen. This was not his will. But because he gave people free will, he can't stop evil from happening."

So you are left with a God who is not all powerful or all knowing or in complete control of his world; a God who means well but can't protect you from bad things or do much for you. You can pray. You can ask God for whatever is on your heart. But when it really matters, you can't count on him to come through for you!

How do you thank a God like that?

God's goodness

How different is the Bible's view of God:

"What do you have that you did not receive? If then you received it, why do you boast as if you did not receive it?" (I Cor. 4:7)

Abilities, talents, opportunities – you didn't create yourself and endow yourself with whatever level of intelligence you have, or with whatever gifts you have that allowed you to get a job. Everything good comes from God, who made you.

*"The LORD looks down from heaven, he sees all the children of man; from where he sits enthroned he looks out on all the inhabitants of the earth, **he who fashions the heart of them all** and observes all their deeds"* (Psalm 33:13-15).

We live in a broken, fallen world. We are not spared the grief and pains of suffering that are common to the human race. But the sadness of our world is not the whole story!

"The child of God who lives in the world of the Bible knows himself to be a very little person in a great and awesome universe. Yet he is given a glimpse of the eternal counsels of the love of God, wherein, before the foundation of the world, the Son took for himself the role of the Lamb to be slain for sinners; wherein the Father pre-ordained to give his chosen ones to the Son as His bride. It is against this backdrop that man, though puny in his ignorance and twisted in his sinfulness, is seen to be the object of God's love" (John Wenham, *The Goodness of God*, p. 48).

Gratitude flourishes in this larger perspective of reality: God is good. Life is a gift. That you are alive today is a gift from God! That you can see, smell, hear, taste and feel; that you have enough food to eat and clothes to wear; that you have a roof over your head to protect you from the wind and rain; that you don't live every day in fear that your family will be attacked by hostile enemies – these are all evidences of God's goodness.

"The LORD is good to all, and his mercy is over all He has made....The eyes of all look to you, and you give them their food in due season. You open your hand; you satisfy the desire of every living thing" (Psalm 145:9, 15-16).

Most of all, that God would love us and provide a Savior for sinful people like us is an infinitely glorious and gracious gift! God does not treat us as our sins deserve or repay us according to our iniquity (Psalm 103). Thanking God for his goodness should be a regular part of your prayers and fellowship with God.

Give thanks

"Oh give thanks to the Lord, for he is good; for his steadfast love endures forever!" (Psalm 118:28-29)

"Make a joyful noise to the LORD, all the earth. Serve the LORD with gladness!

Come into his presence with singing. Know that the LORD, he is God. It is he who made us, and we are his; we are his people, and the sheep of his pasture. **Enter his gates with thanksgiving,** *and his courts with praise! Give thanks to him; bless his name! For the LORD is good; his steadfast love endures forever, and his faithfulness to all generations"* (Psalm 100).

"Continue steadfastly in prayer, being watchful in it **with thanksgiving…** *"* (Colossians 4:2).

"Rejoice always, pray without ceasing, **give thanks in all circumstances,** *for this is the will of God in Christ Jesus for you"* (I Thessalonians 5:16-18).

"Don't be anxious about anything…but in everything by prayer and supplication **with thanksgiving** *let your requests be made known to God…"* (Philippians 4:6).

"Therefore, as you received Christ Jesus the Lord, so walk in him, rooted and built up in him and established in the faith, just as you were taught, **abounding in thanksgiving"** (Colossians 2:6-7).

This is what God wants for you, and this is what he commands, not because he is insecure and needs affirmation. God tells us to give thanks not for his benefit, but for ours. Being thankful produces things in our lives that are good, things like humility and joy and dependence on God. By commanding us to be thankful, God doesn't lay a heavy burden on our shoulders by commanding something unreasonable or something that is extremely difficult to do. Because God is good, he wants what is best for us. Because he is wise, he knows what is best for us.

Unthankful people tend to be unhappy people. Unthankful people are usually not content. They are self-absorbed: "It's all about me!" They are not usually giving or generous people. It's like the world owes them something and hasn't come through for them! They got the short stick in life and it's not fair! Nothing is ever good enough. They can always point out what isn't right in the way they've been treated.

By commanding us to be thankful and to express thanksgiving, God is not just giving good advice or a friendly recommendation. He is telling us what is best for us! However, there are a few things we need to understand about the commands we find in the Bible.

1. **That God commands you to do something does not assume you have the innate ability to do it!**

   "Love the LORD with all your heart, soul, mind and strength. Love your neighbor as yourself" (Luke 10:27). God knows what is true about our hearts. He understands what sin does to us. He knows our inability to do what God commands far better than we do. But he still commands what is in our best interest.

   To a certain degree, you can discipline and train yourself to do what God commands. You can teach your kids to say: "Thank You." You watch as someone gives them a gift and you hear no response come from their mouths. So you say, "What do you say?" And they come out with a bland "thank you." After a while, they figure it out and they will say thanks in the appropriate situations.

   Does that mean they are actually thankful? Of course not. You can teach a parrot to say "thank you!" Saying "thank you" and being thankful are not exactly the same thing!

   When I was a senior in High School, I received a typewriter from my parents for Christmas. I wanted a bike and I got an electric typewriter. In my mind, a bike meant fun, a typewriter meant work. What were they thinking? A typewriter was not what I wanted and I didn't feel very thankful. Selfishness and disappointment in not getting what I wanted was more powerful than any sense of gratitude. But I said, "Thank you. It's just what I needed!" I knew what I was supposed to say. I didn't feel thankful, but I said the words anyway.

   That typewriter got me all the way through college and seminary. I had it up until I was married and we bought our first computer and discovered the beauty of word processing programs!

The typewriter was a good gift. It just took me a while to be thankful for it! (By the way, I was talking to some of our nieces and nephews about college a few years ago and told them that I had to write all my papers with a typewriter since I didn't have a computer. One niece got a puzzled look on her face and asked with all sincerity, "Then how did you get your emails?") My parents, in their wisdom, gave me what they knew I needed, not what I wanted.

I suspect God is like that.

We are commanded by God to give thanks. But what you find in your heart is ingratitude or at best, indifference. Every day of your life there has been air to breathe, food to eat, and clothes to wear. So you don't even think that all the things you enjoy every day are an undeserved gift from a kind and giving God.

So *saying* "thank you" is one thing. Being thankful requires a change of heart. You can't change your heart by telling yourself you should be more thankful. You need God to change your heart. And God is at work doing just that! He has given you a new heart with a new ability to do what God commands. He has given you the Holy Spirit to change your heart's desires. You can assume that God will work in your life to make you thankful, because God wants what is best for you.

God commands us to be thankful. And God works in us to change our hearts so we actually become more thankful. But still, growing in gratitude won't just sort of happen to you if you just wait for a while.

There is a way to grow in this area: You can think, remember, and consider what God has done for you!

2. **There are always reasons for gratitude**

*"Oh give thanks to the Lord, **for** he is good; **for** his steadfast love endures forever!"* (Psalm 118:28-29). The way to develop a more grateful heart, the way to grow in expressing thanks in prayer is to think about what God has done for you.

One of my daughters has been writing a blog for a few years. This year she decided she would try to think of one thing to be thankful for on each day of the year. She's half way through the year. It has been fun to read her list as she reflects on God's goodness to her in so many ways and expresses thanks.

If you remember the words of this praise song, you have been around for a while: "Count your blessings, name them one by one, and it will surprise you what the LORD has done." That's not just good, practical advice. That is what the psalmists encourage when they call us to give thanks to God:

*"Bless the LORD, O my soul, and **forget not** all His benefits"* (Psalm 103:2). The psalmist then begins to recount the many ways God has blessed us: *"Who forgives all your iniquity, who heals all your diseases, who redeems your life from the pit, who crowns you with steadfast love and mercy, who satisfies you with good so that your youth is renewed like the eagle's"* (Psalm 103:3-5). The psalmist goes on to say God doesn't treat me as I deserve. He has loved me with a steadfast love. He has removed my sins from me as far as east is from west.

To "forget not" all God's benefits is not a trite comment. That's a serious command, which will produce deep joy in your life as you give attention to doing what God commands – being thankful.

"Let them thank the LORD for his steadfast love, for his wondrous works to the children of men…" (Psalm 107:21). In Psalm 107, the psalmist recounts how God had rescued people, provided for people, delivered them in times of trouble.

There are always reasons for being thankful.

3. Gratitude needs a direction: it is relational.

For reasons I can't quite explain, I watched the Academy Awards program on television this year. It was interesting to hear so many expressions of thanks: "I want to thank my producer, my director, my mother, my colleagues, the academy for its reasonable insight in choosing me for this award this year over all the others…" Those receiving the awards all seemed to recognize that they didn't get to this point in life all by themselves. Friends helped them. People gave them opportunities. Family members sacrificed so they could work (I was pleased to hear so many men thank their wives).

When an atheist is in a car accident and survives, I imagine the words "thank you" cross his mind. Someone who knows he almost died suddenly feels a tremendous sense of gratitude. But who does he thank? Does he thank the car manufacturer, the guy who worked on his brakes, the highway department that put the barrier there that kept his car from going off the cliff? The answer is probably "all of the above."

If you don't believe God exists or if you think God is a kind of power that pervades the universe (not a person you can know and relate to), God will not figure into your expressions of thanks very often. But I assume even an atheist feels thankful at times. He just doesn't know who to thank!

Those spontaneous feelings of gratitude – that he should be thankful – are hints that there is a God in the universe. If something feels like a gift, that's because there is a Giver:

> "Every meal, every pleasure, every possession, every bit of sun, every night's sleep, every moment of health and safety, everything else that sustains and enriches life, <u>is a divine gift</u>. And how abundant those gifts are!" (J.I. Packer, *Knowing God*, p. 147)

You can feel thankful for the gifts you receive in life; you can honestly feel that so many things in your life are undeserved gifts from God; you can value those gifts and appreciate them very much without thinking much of the Giver of every good gift or telling him "Thank you"! Expressing thanks implies a relationship: there is someone who has given. You have received. It feels right to tell them thank you!

When I give my wife some little thing, or when I give my kids something for Christmas, I want to hear them say "thank you." I know my motives are selfish: I want recognition for my generosity and kindness and thoughtfulness. I want to know that they recognize my goodness.

There can be a selfish motivation in wanting someone to express gratitude for what you have done for them. But giving and receiving implies a relationship. And receiving sincere thanks for a gift given kind of completes the giving – it adds joy to the giving. A gift is something that is freely given, not out of obligation or a grudging sense of duty. Giving a gift is not a business transaction (as in, "If I give you this, I expect you to give me something of equal value."). I give gifts to people I love because it's a way of expressing love and it's a way of enjoying the relationship.

God doesn't command us to give thanks because he needs our approval and affirmation and recognition. He commands us to be thankful so we will understand something about reality – that we are not self-made, independent, self-reliant people. Ultimately, God wants us to express thanks so we will grow in terms of knowing him, the giver of every good and perfect gift.

It might not sound spiritual to talk about material blessings (physical things like food, water, a roof over your head, clothes to wear, a way to get to work). But the fact is, God put us in a physical, material world. To live for another week, you need food and water. And it would be nice to have a roof over your head and clothes to wear when it's cold outside. We live in a culture that depends on cars and trucks to get to the grocery stores and to work. Food, clothes, a house, and a car to drive are not good or evil in themselves. If you receive them with gratitude as gifts from God, they are blessings from God! Giving thanks for these simple daily things is a basic, foundational part of prayer.

All of these material things like food, water, clothes, and a house pale in comparison to the gift of grace in Jesus Christ. What you need most today is forgiveness and peace with God. If you have all the food and drink and clothes and stuff you want, but don't have God's grace in Jesus Christ, you are poor! All these other things are temporary. Your life in this present world will end. What you need most is the life that is found in Jesus Christ.

But knowing that God has shown you mercy and grace in Christ, and knowing that whatever else you have in life comes from God, you have a lot for which to be thankful! If thanksgiving is grounded in gifts received from a person who cares for you, that implies a personal relationship.

Experiencing God's goodness

How have bad things that you've experienced kept you from seeing the goodness of God or kept you from being grateful for the good things God has given you?

"There are indeed terrible evils in the world, but if we are to see things in proportion, we dare not dwell exclusively on them. There may be times when we feel the whole earth to be a vile place, and we never want to open a newspaper or watch a news program again. Yet to think of it in these terms patently represents only a half-truth. Almost all of us have a host of memories, if we care to summon them, of exquisite and breath-taking pleasures – the joys of friendship and humor, of home and love, the joys of adventure, the joys of the natural world, the joys of mental discovery, of literature, of drama. …If we once take our sin seriously, and extract all the evils caused by sin from our view of the world, we have to admit that most of what is left looks like something worthy of a good and glorious Creator" (John Wenham, *The Goodness of God*, p. 48).

Being Thankful In Advance

When the Apostle Paul invites us to approach God in prayer, he says, *The Lord is at hand"* (Philippians 4:5b). When something is "at hand," it is close or about to happen. Paul says God is not far away and hard to reach. He is close to us, available to us, welcoming when we approach him.

"The Lord is at hand; do not be anxious about anything, but in everything by prayer and supplication **with thanksgiving** *let your requests be made known to God"* (Philippians 4:5b-6).

Even as you lay your requests before God, you can know that God's goodness doesn't depend on God doing exactly what you ask of him. Faith involves trusting that God loves you, that God knows what you need, that God wants you to ask, and that God cares about you. Faith involves trust that God is infinitely wise – he will do what is best for you.

You don't have to be anxious about difficult things you're facing. That is easy to say and much harder to do when you're the one facing some difficult, seemingly impossible situation, but this is how we are invited to live before God! Instead of being anxious, take your concerns to God "with thanksgiving" – being thankful even as you pour out your requests before God.

Tell him what's on your heart. Thank him that you can call him Father, that he loves you, that he will do what is best for you, that he will not leave you or forsake you, that nothing in creation can separate you from his love.

You don't have to pretend that everything is good. God never asks you to believe that bad things are really good things in disguise! Evil is always evil. Wrong things that happen to you are wrong. Sin is always displeasing to God. Christians aren't asked to pretend that everything is really good. We are asked to believe that God is good! There is no evil in God. God has no dark side that delights in hurting people. He is good always in everything he does. Why he tolerates evil in his world remains a mystery that won't be explained until the story of this world is finished. In the meantime, we are asked to trust him and believe that he is working in all circumstances, even the wrong and sinful things that he allows people to do, to accomplish the greatest possible good.

Remember, your story isn't finished yet! You can't see clearly what God is doing. You don't know how things that seem bad and things that really are bad that happen to you will be used by God for good in your life when it is all done. But you can know and rest in the truth that God knows what he is doing and he is working to accomplish the greatest good in your life.

When you believe God is good, you can be thankful, no matter what circumstances you face.

"Give thanks unto the LORD, for he is good...O that men would praise the LORD for his goodness, and for his wonderful works to the children of men!" (Psalm 107:1,31)

You have experienced the goodness of God every day of your life. Can you tell God "thank you"?

PART V

"Forgive us our debts as we forgive our debtors"

E CAN'T GET AROUND THE FACT that we are sinful people. We sin against God in words, thoughts, and actions. We don't do what God commands us to do and we do things he commands us not to do. In the process, we sin against other people. In that sense, we are debtors. We owe a relational debt to God (we should honor and obey him and we fail to do that) and we create relational debts with other people by not loving them as we should.

Without confession and repentance, we end up bitter, full of resentments, and hardened in our attitudes. We become defensive, feeling like we have to prove to everyone that we are right about what we say and do.

Jesus taught us to include confession and repentance in our prayers, and the psalms give us some wonderful models of prayers of confession.

Chapter 10

Confession Isn't Enough

HEN I PASTORED A CHURCH, that had a regular weekly prayer meeting, there was a man who closed his prayer every week by saying, "…and forgive us our sins, for they are many." I understand what he meant, but I sometimes wish I had asked him, "Do you ever get more specific than that?"

When Jesus taught his disciples to include confession of sin in their prayers – *"Forgive us our debts…"* – he did not mean we should tack on these words to our prayers as a kind of general request for forgiveness.

Psalm 139 ends with a rather frightening request: *"Search me, O God, and know my heart! Try me and know my thoughts! And see if there be any grievous way in me, and lead me in the way everlasting."* As he meditates on the depths of God's knowledge, he is aware that God knows his heart far more clearly than he does. We tend to be blind to the desires, attitudes, and assumptions that shape our choices. While we are aware of some of our sins, we are not usually aware of the heart attitudes that drive our sinful words and behavior. The psalmist is open to having God show him the truth about his thoughts and attitudes.

What about you? Are you willing to have God show you what's in your heart? If you're honest, you have to admit that you're not all that excited about the prospect of discovering the truth about the depths of sin in your heart. I'm with you on that one! I can't say I'm as excited about knowing the *"grievous way"* in my heart as the psalmist seems to be. I like the philosophy "ignorance is bliss" or "what I don't know can't hurt me."

When Adam and Eve sinned against God in the Garden of Eden, they felt shame and tried to hide. That's what sinners do! Sinful people don't want to face the truth about their sin. We avoid facing the truth about our hearts.

That's why the Westminster Confession of Faith says repentance is an "evangelical grace." The word "evangelical" comes from the word "evangel" which means "gospel." So repentance is a gospel grace. That I would ever truly repent is evidence that God is at work in me, that his Spirit has created new life in me. When I find in my heart a willingness to repent and face the truth about my sin, that should move me with joy! I would never be willing to face the depths of sin in my heart unless God was at work in my life. A willingness to repent honestly is an evidence of God's saving presence!

Gospel grace

Repentance starts with seeing the truth about your sin – seeing it as an offense against God, as contrary to God's nature, and as rebellion against his righteous commands. Repentance is a gospel *grace*. It is not something you work up in yourself or accomplish by your own determination and resolve. It is a work of grace; an undeserved gift given to you by God. The inclination to repent, the willingness to repent, and actually repenting are all something God stirs up in you.

At the same time, confessing our sin and repenting of it is a battle. Something in our hearts resists admitting the truth about our sin. Even talking about sin and our need for confession and repentance sounds negative. You may be thinking, "Isn't there a more pleasant subject we could talk about?"

Confessing the truth about your heart and repenting of sin is intolerable apart from the gospel. Shame is a powerful feeling! Sin produces not only a sense of guilt, but feelings of shame and dirtiness. That's why we hide the truth about our hearts, deny our sin is real or stuff it down deep inside. Guilt is knowing you have done something wrong. Shame is the feeling that something is wrong with *you*.

But if you know and believe that Jesus bore the guilt of your sin and that he bore your shame in his death in your place, you can come to him and face the truth about your heart. You can know that God, in his amazing love for you, is working to set you free from the slavery sin creates in your life.

Repentance is the flip side of faith. If you know you are loved and accepted you don't have to be afraid of what other people think about you if they know the truth about your sin. All that matters in the end is that God knows the truth and that he forgives you and restores you when you come to him in repentance.

Facing the truth

Repentance involves being sorry for your sin, grieving over your sin, hating it, turning from it to God, and pleading with God to change your heart. Repentance involves depending on God to give you new desires that will produce changed behavior.

Because God is for you, you can face the truth about your sinful heart.

Prayer is about intimacy with God – knowing and being known in an environment of security. When you are confident that he loves you and accepts you, you don't have to hide from God in fear. Grace sets you free to trust God. You don't have to be afraid of what you'll discover if God shows you what's in your heart. He is not against you. He is for you. He proved this by giving his own Son to bear the punishment for sin in our place.

Suppose you find the courage to pray: "Father, I want to know you. I want to be thirsty and hungry for you. I want to delight my soul in you. Would you search me, O God, and know my heart! Would you try me and know my thoughts! Would you see if there is any grievous way in me, and lead me in the way everlasting. Show me what is in my heart and change my heart!" How would God answer that prayer?

What if later in the day, after you've asked God to show you the truth about the sin in your heart, you have a disagreement with your wife. In the process, you say something that you know hurts her feelings. You start to feel bad about what you said, so you come to her and say, "I'm sorry. Please forgive me." But instead of quickly forgiving you, suppose she finds the courage to say, "What does that mean? What are you asking me to forgive? It would help if you could tell me specifically what you did that needs my forgiveness."

You could say, "Well, I'm sorry I hurt your feelings. I shouldn't have said what I said and hurt your feelings."

She thinks about that, and says, "I'm still not clear on what you think you did that needs forgiving. Are you saying 'you're sorry' because I took offense at what you said…that I took it the wrong way? So it's really my fault that I feel hurt and I shouldn't be so sensitive? Tell me what exactly it is you did that needs my forgiveness?"

That kind of honest probing reply brings up defensiveness and anger. That's been my experience. When I asked my wife to forgive me, she, being a sweet Christian woman, was obligated to say, "Okay, I forgive you." I took that to mean the discussion was now closed. After all, if you forgive someone, you don't bring the offense up again, right? So, time after time, I would shut down all discussion by quickly asking my wife to forgive me. In this way, I was not forced to look at what was really driving my heart.

Finally, a friend suggested that instead of asking Margaret to forgive me when I knew I had offended her, I should say something like: "I am sorry I hurt you by what I said. Can you help me understand how my words hurt you?" My friend suggested I should listen and think about what she's saying without defending myself or trying to explain why what I said or did was reasonable.

When I began to really listen to my wife, I began to see how I had hurt her in ways I had never intended or considered. It drove me to Christ in repentance at a level I had never experienced before. I didn't want to face the truth about my sin. I did all I could to avoid having to see what was in my heart. But God in his grace let me see what was there so I would understand more clearly how desperately I needed him to change my heart.

Underneath the surface

Repentance is a gospel grace! Because God loves us, he wants what is best for us – he wants to set us free from controlling patterns of sin that remain in our hearts. And the first step is seeing the truth about what is driving our sinful thoughts, words and actions.

If you confess sin generally, you never get around to facing the sinful heart attitudes that are behind the surface sins!

There is a great statement in the *Westminster Confession of Faith* about being specific when it comes to confessing sin:

"Men ought not to content themselves with a general repentance, but it is every man's duty to endeavor to repent of his particular sins, particularly" (WCF chapter 15, section 5).

If it would help, you can substitute the word "specific" for the word "particular" – it is our duty to repent of specific sins, specifically. General confession – "forgive me for my many sins" – won't force you to see how desperately you need a Savior! It is a gospel grace when God shows you specifically what is in your heart and drives you to repentance for specific sins.

How will God show you the truth about your sin and lead you to repentance? If you belong to him, he will work in you to show you your sin and lead you to repentance. A lack of repentance over time should make you question whether or not God's Spirit is in you at all.

How will God do it?

Sometimes by bringing conviction of sin to your conscience. Sometimes through a friend, a parent, your spouse – someone who tells you something you need to hear. Sometimes it takes more.

David's sin

As you read the account of David's life in the Bible, you can see God working to bring David to an awareness of his sin in different ways:

Early in his life, when Saul was pursuing him to take his life, David had an opportunity to kill Saul. The king was alone in a cave, and David crept up and cut off a corner of Saul's robe. David's men were convinced God had delivered Saul into David's hands so David could kill his enemy. But David was conscience stricken after cutting off a corner of Saul's robe. He felt guilty. By showing Saul even that small token of disrespect, David felt he had sinned against God's anointed king. He called out to Saul and confessed what he had done. Without any prompting from someone close to him, David's conscience convicted him of sin.

Another time he was about to kill a man for being insolent, and the man's wife, Abigail, came and pleaded with him to not do what he was about to do. God used an honest person to show David his sin before it went farther.

But another time, it took a major confrontation.

There is a note in our English Bible translations before verse one of Psalm 51: *"To the choirmaster. A psalm of David, when Nathan the prophet went to him, after he had gone in to Bathsheba."* That's the setting for this great psalm of repentance. The background is found in II Samuel 11 and Nathan's confrontation of David is found in II Samuel 12.

It's a familiar story: David was at the high point of kingly success. He didn't have to go out to war any more to fight Israel's enemies. He sent his generals out to fight and he stayed at home in Jerusalem.

"It happened, late one afternoon, when David arose from his couch and was walking on the roof of the king's house, that he saw from the roof a woman bathing, and the woman was very beautiful. And David sent and inquired about the women. And one said, 'Is not this Bathsheba, the daughter of Eliam, the wife of Uriah the Hittite?' " (II Samuel 11:2-3).

Uriah was one of David's faithful friends! So this wasn't the wife of a stranger. This was the wife of a man who loved David and had stood by him faithfully for many years.

"So David sent messengers and took her, and she came to him, and he lay with

her....then she returned to her house. And the woman conceived, and she sent and told David, "I am pregnant" (II Samuel 11:4-5).

Oops. This is the kind of thing that causes national scandals! Think of a past president: "I did not have relations with that woman…" Or a prominent governor forced to confess his infidelity to his wife when the truth about his affair in Argentina came to light. The list goes on and on including prominent pastors and Christian leaders.

David knew this was the kind of scandal that could ruin a good career. So he did what any king or high profile person with power would do. He tried to cover it up. He brought Uriah home from battle, thinking he would spend a little time with his wife and everyone, including Uriah, would then think the baby was Uriah's. That didn't work. So David arranged to have Uriah killed in battle. He had him placed in the hottest part of the battle and arranged for his fellow soldiers to pull back so the enemy would overwhelm him and kill him.

David didn't take a sword and strike down Uriah with his own hands. But it was still murder. David just used enemy soldiers to do the killing for him.

When Uriah was dead, David would take the grieving widow to be his wife, which would appear to be a wonderful expression of love for Uriah. David would look like a faithful friend. And when Bathsheba bore a child, it would all look normal. That was David's plan.

Displeasing the Lord

"But the thing that David had done displeased the LORD" (II Samuel 11:27b).

Why did it not displease David? He is called a "man after God's own heart!" Read the psalms he wrote and you will see a man who clearly loved God deeply!

I have heard people say, David must not have been "saved" after all because someone who was saved would never do what he did. That strikes me as rather naïve! What Jeremiah says about the human heart applies to "saved" people as well as it applies to "unsaved" people: "The heart is deceitful above all things, and desperately wicked: who can know it?" (Jeremiah 17:9, KJV).

If you are honest about the sin that is still there in your heart, what David did shouldn't surprise you. The seeds of all kinds of sin are there in our hearts, too!

The interesting thing in this story is that David seemed to be oblivious to his sin in this whole thing. Adultery, lies, cover up, plotting the death of a man who trusted and loved him, conspiring with friends to carry out murder – and there doesn't seem to be a guilty conscience!

It helps to remember that we know only part of the story that God has chosen to reveal in Scripture. We're not told that David felt guilty about any of this! That doesn't necessarily mean he didn't have feelings of guilt or shame. What we do know is that David was not openly repentant. There was no public confession of sin. The truth was buried and ignored.

The amazing thing is that this story is told at all. If the men who wrote the Bible were writing a Jewish history for posterity or a document to convince people to believe what they believed, why not suppress this story? If they wrote the Bible to attract people to the God they believed in, why not just present David as a hero, a great statesman, a good king? After all, a *"man after God's heart"* doesn't do this kind of stuff!

David's conscience didn't seem to convict him. Those who knew what David had done (whoever helped him bring Bathsheba to his house) and those who obeyed David and made sure Uriah was killed didn't come and talk to him about how wrong he had been to do what he did. David was the king. Kings do whatever they want! They're above the laws that govern other people!

No, they're not.

"And the LORD sent Nathan to David. He came to him and said, to him, 'There were two men in a certain city, the one rich and the other poor. The rich man had very many flocks and herds, but the poor man had nothing but one little ewe lamb which he had bought. And he brought it up, and it grew up with him and with his children. It used to eat of his morsel and drink from his

cut and lie in his arms, and it was like a daughter to him. Now there came a traveler to the rich man, and he was unwilling to take one of his own flock or herd to prepare for the guest who had come to him, but he took the poor man's lamb and prepared it for the man who had come to him.' Then David's anger was greatly kindled against the man, and he said to Nathan, 'As the LORD lives, the man who has done this deserves to die, and he shall restore the lamb fourfold, because he did this thing, and because he had no pity.'

"Nathan said to David, 'You are the man! Thus says the LORD, the God of Israel, 'I anointed you king over Israel, and I delivered you out of the hand of Saul. And I gave you your master's house and your master's wives into your arms and gave you the house of Israel and of Judah. And if this were too little, I would add to you as much more. Why have you despised the word of the LORD, to do what is evil in his sight? You have struck down Uriah the Hittite with the sword and have killed him with the sword of the Ammonites. Now therefore the sword shall never depart from your house, because you have despised me and have taken the wife of Uriah the Hittite to be your wife...'

"...David said to Nathan, 'I have sinned against the LORD.' And Nathan said to David, 'The LORD also has put away your sin; you shall not die. Nevertheless, because by this deed you have utterly scorned the LORD, the child who is born to you shall die'..." (II Samuel 12:1-13).

This is the background to Psalm 51. *"To the choirmaster. A psalm of David, when Nathan the prophet went to him, after he had gone in to Bathsheba."*

Consequences of sin

He was blind to his offense against God until God confronted him with the truth. But that David was really a man after God's heart is evident in the way he responded. You find no attempt to deny the truth, no attempts to excuse his behavior, no anger at Nathan for daring to speak so boldly to the king. You find a broken heart and more than that, a deep desire to be right with God!

"Have mercy on me, O God, according to your steadfast love; according to your abundant mercy blot out my transgressions. Wash me thoroughly from my iniquity, and cleanse me from my sin! For I know my transgressions, and my sin is ever before me. Against you, you only, have I sinned and done what is evil in your sight, so you may be justified in your words and blameless in your judgment" (Psalm 51:1-4).

What words did David have in mind? What judgment was he referring to? He's talking about the words God spoke to him through the prophet Nathan. God announced judgment: The child will die. The sword will not depart from your house.

Bathsheba was probably the daughter of a war hero named Eliam, who was the son of Ahithophel, who seems to have been unable to forgive David for what he had done. Ahithophel later counseled David's son, Absalom, to defile his father's wives. It also seems that many people in the nation were unable to forgive David and joined Absalom's rebellion against David. We'll come back to this in the next two chapters.

Have mercy on me, O God

To ask for mercy, honestly and sincerely, is to admit that you deserve something different from God than what you're asking of him. You deserve nothing good from God. You deserve his wrath and displeasure. You deserve punishment because you have offended a good, loving and holy God who has treated you with kindness!

What had God done for David? He was a shepherd, a nobody, just one of the many sons of a man named Jesse. He was not the oldest or the greatest. But God raised him up and anointed him to be the future king of Israel to replace King Saul. God protected him for years as Saul tried to kill him. God gave him the kingdom. God gave him wives, children, wealth, victory in battle.

As he begins this prayer, David is keenly aware that he has repaid God's goodness with contempt. How did God describe David's sin? God said, *"You have despised the word of the Lord....you have despised me....you have utterly scorned the Lord."*

Most of us don't think of our sin in those terms! We say,

"I made a poor choice."

"I made a mistake."

"I know it was wrong but..."

If God said David despised and utterly scorned him in the sinful choices he made, could the same thing be said of us when we sin? I don't think David consciously chose to treat God with contempt. He didn't think of his choices as scorning or despising God any more than we do when we sin. He loved God. But God's evaluation of his behavior revealed heart attitudes that David didn't see until God confronted him through Nathan.

David continues: *"For I know my transgressions, and my sin is ever before me. Against you, you only, have I sinned and done what is evil in your sight"* (Psalm 51:4).

He is not denying the fact that he had sinned against Uriah, against Bathsheba, and against the nation. He had hurt a lot of people by his sin. But ultimately, *all sin is against God.*

You can't sin against your wife or your husband or your mother or father or child or friend without at the same time and in a deeper way sin against God!

Jesus said the greatest commandment is this: "You shall love the Lord your God with all your heart, soul, mind and strength. The second greatest commandment is: You shall love your neighbor as yourself" (Matthew 22:37-38). You can't break the second greatest commandment without breaking the great commandment at the same time. God made that other person you sinned against. God commands you to love them. When you failed to love your neighbor as yourself, you despised God's commandment, devalued someone made in his image and likeness, and in doing all that, scorned God.

We will never confess our sins well, or repent well of our sins if we don't see our sin for what it is at that level!

Honest confession

Suppose you have a "disagreement" with your wife, and you get angry. You think she's being unfair. She's exaggerating. She's not giving you much credit. And out of you come some hurtful, cutting words.

Your conscience starts to bother you as you cool down. You work up the willingness to go to her and say, "I'm sorry for the way I spoke to you. I used words that hurt you. I was wrong to let my anger be an excuse for hurting you. I'm sorry, would you help me understand how my words have impacted you?"

She hesitates to respond and looks at you with what you take to be suspicion, and you get a bit miffed about that! Here you are, doing the godly man thing! You humbled yourself and made yourself vulnerable, and she responded with a lack of trust.

It could be that prior experience has made her gun shy! What you took to be suspicion and lack of trust in your genuineness could be fear. Can she trust that if she tells you the truth about how you have impacted her, you won't turn on her with more hurtful words or punish her in some way (maybe the silent treatment)?

Suppose she tells you the truth, like Nathan told David, and you hear it and feel convicted of your sin before God. What would confession and repentance in prayer look like or sound like?

How about this: "God, I confess that I was angry at my wife. I said some hurtful things to her. Please forgive me." Is that sufficient? No, it's too general. What about repenting of *particular sins, particularly?* How has your anger been sin against God? How have you despised God in the way you treated your wife?

This would be a good time to pray, *"Search me, O God and know my heart."* What if you prayed something like this:

"God, I see the tip of the iceberg of my sin. I see the stuff above the surface of the water but I don't see how big and how dangerous the iceberg is under the water. I see some of my sin, but I don't know my own heart.

"In my anger, I feel justified, like I have good reasons for being angry. I feel justified in speaking out of anger when I feel wronged.

"But in my willingness to use words to hurt my wife, I have not valued the wife you gave me. I have not loved her as Jesus loved his bride. I have disregarded the gift you've given me – this woman you gave me to be my bride. In doing that, I have despised you. I have acted like you were unwise and not good in uniting me to her in marriage."

Now that is a lot more particular. Would that kind of honest prayer change your concept of what it means to need God's mercy and grace? If you think your sin is small and really not a big deal, you'll never think you need mercy from God.

David said, "I need mercy. I need a thorough washing from my sin. I am guilty as charged. I need you, God, to cleanse me in a way I can't cleanse myself. I know that I have done what is evil in your sight, so you are right to condemn me for my sin. But I plead for mercy!

Is confessing enough?

There is a big difference between admitting your sin, confessing it (even publicly), and repenting before God. You are well acquainted with public figures who have been forced to make a public confession of wrongdoing. Maybe you watched South Carolina Governor Mark Sanford confessing his sin on television. It was pretty good as far as confessions go. He said, "I have been unfaithful to my wife. I have been having an affair with a family friend from Argentina. What I have done has hurt a lot of people – my wife, my children, my family, and the State of South Carolina." He was honest about what he had done.

But confessing sin and repenting of it are not exactly the same thing. One of my friends used to say, "I can't tell if he's confessing or bragging!" When you hear some public confessions, it's hard to tell!

There is a biblical principle about confession that can be summarized like this: private sin should be confessed privately. But scandalous sin, public sin, should be confessed publicly. Sin should be acknowledged before those who have been hurt by the sin. But again, there is a difference between confession and biblical repentance.

There is therapeutic freedom that comes with admitting the wrong you have done. You feel relief when you honestly confess your failures and struggles and no longer have to hide. What you'll often find is that when you get honest, people are willing to accept and forgive you. That is liberating. Confession can bring great relief.

Real repentance

But confession alone won't change you. That's not what biblical confession and repentance are about. Confession involves acknowledging sin and admitting you are guilty. No excuses. No defense of your behavior. No rationalizing what you have done. Confession involves telling the truth about your sin.

Repentance continues where confession has begun. Repentance requires a recognition of your need for mercy – you need God to do what you can't do for yourself. You need God to cleanse and change your heart. Repentance involves pleading with him to do that! Repentance involves a deep desire to be right with God – caring more about how your sin has impacted him than about how it has hurt other people.

Certainly your sin affects other people, but ultimately it is against God. When God gives you the gospel grace of repentance, you care more about how your sin has affected God than you care about your reputation or what other people think of you.

The longer you walk with God, the more you will see the truth about the sin in your heart that produces sin in your thoughts, words and actions. At the same time, the gospel will become more beautiful. God's love for you does not depend on your goodness. He knows your heart. He knows you intimately. Before a word is on your lips, he knows it completely. But he still chose to lavish grace on you! And it is his love that leads him to expose your sin in order to set you free.

Prayer is about intimacy with God, knowing and being known in a secure relationship of love. When you know God has provided a Savior and that Jesus has paid the debt for your sin in full, you are set free to be honest about your sin. Jesus carried your guilt and removed your shame when he died in your place on the cross.

When you go to God with confession, may he give you the grace of repentance.

Chapter 11

A Broken and Contrite Heart

*T*HIS COULD ONLY HAPPEN IN A DREAM, but go with me on this. Imagine it's August in Florida. It's Saturday morning. The humidity level is about 95 percent. The temperature is already in the mid-80s. You are outside, with the mid-morning sun burning down on you as you finish mowing the lawn. And you smile as you think to yourself, "Ahh, this is great! This is exactly why I moved to Florida." You're covered with dust and dirt and yard clippings and glad no one is close enough to get a whiff of your sweat soaked shirt.

Suddenly, a black suburban pulls into your driveway and a couple big men in black suits and sunglasses invite you to step into the car. You ask if you can go clean up first but they bluntly respond, "Sorry, no time for that," and escort you to the back seat of the suburban. No explanation is given as they put you in the back seat. After a short drive, they deliver you in your stinky, dirty, sweat-soaked, finery to a meeting with the President of the United States. Television cameras are rolling. Everyone you see is wearing a nice tailored suit except you.

How do you think you'd feel as you stood there before the President and all the news cameras? Out of place? Embarrassed? Uncomfortable? Ashamed?

Something like this actually happened to the Old Testament prophet, Isaiah.

In a vision, he found himself standing before God's throne in heaven. The manifestation of God that he could see was blindingly beautiful. God was surrounded by terrifying angels and there was smoke and an earthquake.

"And I said: Woe is me! For I am lost; for I am a man of unclean lips, and I dwell in the midst of a people of unclean lips; for my eyes have seen the King, the LORD of hosts" (Isaiah 6:5).

An ordinary man, suddenly and unexpectedly found himself standing before God in all his majesty and holiness. He felt dirty, terribly uncomfortable, terrified, and deeply ashamed!

When we come to worship on a Sunday morning, we gather in a comfortable, air-conditioned room, with a group of people we know. We say we are gathering in the presence of God to worship him, but we can't see him. We can't see God in all his holy splendor or those terrifying angels around his throne. Instead, we see our friends, sitting politely nearby looking quite proper.

On most Sunday mornings in most churches, people rush in at the last minute. Some look like they just rolled out of bed. Some look a bit upset because they came in late and had to sit closer to the front because the back row was already full. Some even look a bit upset because they can't believe someone took their seat.

What do you see when you walk into your church building? Most church buildings in this country look a lot like a concert hall or theatre or lecture hall: all the seats are arranged to face a platform. So it's easy to assume we, the people who gather, are the audience watching a few people giving a kind of religious performance. We're spectators.

But in biblical thinking – every person in the congregation is on the platform. There is only one person in the audience. The musicians and the pastor are there to help you by reminding you of your lines. The pastor calls you to worship: *"Come, let us worship and bow down…"* The musicians invite you to respond to God by giving you words to express praise to the King. As he preaches, the pastor reminds you of who the King is and what it means to belong to him by God's grace. In biblical imagery, God, the King, is the audience. He is the one watching as we worship.

If you really understood that you are sitting and standing and kneeling in the presence of God when you gather for worship with God's people, how would that make you feel? It might feel like you showed up in dirty, sweaty, stinky yard-working clothes for an interview with the president! But the contrast is far, far greater than that.

God is infinitely holy. He is absolutely all-knowing. No word you spoke, nothing you did, no thought, no desire, no attitude you had this day, yesterday, or any other day of your life is unknown to him or hidden from his sight. Before him we are absolutely laid bare. It is impossible to hide…anything.

It's no wonder that in older traditions in the Church, worship began with personal confession of sin. The *Didache* (a document that is not in the New Testament but dates from the first century, giving instructions for the church based on apostolic teaching) has this line: "In church confess your sins, and do not come to your prayer with a guilty conscience" (*Didache* 4:14).

What you need

What do you, a sinner, need most when you stand before God? You need a Savior! And that is where worship has to take us: to a Savior for sinners. God pardons those who come to him in repentance and faith. God does not treat us as our sin deserves or repay us according to our iniquity. In love, he has shown us grace and mercy. That's why some of the New Testament letters begin like this: *"Grace to you and peace from God our Father and the Lord Jesus Christ"* (II Corinthians 1:2). Before we say anything else, we need to know that God forgives us and welcomes us!

There should be a kind of gospel flow to the worship service. In some ways, a worship service is a kind of gospel re-enactment. It moves from confession of sin to a reminder of pardon. Then it moves to praise and thanksgiving. When you are assured of pardon for your sin, the result should be joyful expressions of thanksgiving and praise, a new willingness to hear God speaking to you through his Word, and a renewed commitment to give your life to him in obedient service.

Only God can forgive sins. And for those who know they are sinners, this is the starting point of worship. God loves truth, so if we're going to worship him honestly, if we're going to sing hymns and songs that talk about love for God and devotion to him, we need to start by being honest about the sin that is there in our hearts.

If you are going to ask God to forgive your sin, you need to be aware of what your sin is. You need to be specific: what exactly do you need God to forgive? How have you sinned against him?

As we saw in the last chapter, King David had been brought suddenly to an almost overwhelming awareness of how deeply he had offended God by his sin. As he begins to pour out his heart before God in Psalm 51, there is a very keen awareness of what his sin deserved. David did not offer God a general prayer of confession – "Please forgive me if I have sinned." He was honest about his sin.

You have probably had people apologize to you in a very general way: "If I have offended you or upset you, I am sorry." That's not very helpful and not very sincere. If someone is coming to you to ask your forgiveness, you want them to be specific with you. You want to know that they truly understand specifically what was offensive or hurtful. And for the good of our own souls, we need to learn to repent of "particular sins particularly!"

David was guilty of adultery, murder, and covering up his scandalous sin. Through the prophet Nathan, God said to David, *"You have despised my word… you have despised me…you have utterly scorned me…"* David didn't defend himself. He didn't offer excuses. You see the truth of the Bible's claim that David was a man after God's heart in the way David responded: he was contrite, that is, he was genuinely sorry for what his sin had done to God. In David's case, his sin was public. His confession needed to be public for David's own spiritual wellbeing and to teach others about God's grace.

You also see in Psalm 51 a genuine repentance. David turned from his sin toward God. More than anything, he wanted to be restored to a right relationship with God. His repentance made it clear that he did not have the power in himself to change his heart. He came to God in dependence, asking God to change his heart.

David's prayer

Let's look at the words David used in his prayer.

First, notice the words he used to describe sin:

*"Have mercy on me, O God, according to your steadfast love; according to your abundant mercy blot out my **transgressions**.*

*"Wash me thoroughly from my **iniquity**, and cleanse me from my sin!*

*"For I know my **transgressions**, and my sin is ever before me.*

"Against you, you only, have I sinned and done what is evil in your sight, so that you may be justified in your words and blameless in your judgment."

That's quite a list: transgressions, iniquity, sin, evil. To understand what he's saying, we need to define those words.

A *transgression* is a violation of a norm or standard that is done knowingly, not by accident. David did what he knew was wrong. He crossed a moral boundary that he knew God had established clearly.

The word, *iniquity*, means to twist or bend something that is straight or to deviate from a standard.

Sin means to fall short or to miss the mark. Sin is an offense that disqualifies. It is a relational term – it is an offense against someone with whom you have a relationship, ultimately, against God.

Evil is a term most of us rarely use to describe our actions, thoughts or desires. We don't like to think of anything we say or do as evil. For something to be evil means it is devoid of good – it is unrighteous.

Cry for mercy

David is standing deep in a hole, dug by his own choices, looking up and seeing his need for God in a way someone who doesn't see his sin could ever understand. And he pleads with God, *"Have mercy."* He's asking God to show him favor that he has no right to demand or claim. He appeals to God's character when he asks for mercy, *"according to your loving kindness."* He knows God is full of unfailing love. He pleads for *"abundant mercy."* God's mercy is more than compassion for someone who is hurting. He shows mercy even to people who spit in his face. By crying out for mercy, David is admitting his crimes and acknowledging the punishment he deserves. He can't demand forgiveness from God. He can only plead.

Notice the petitions he uses as he asks God to forgive him: *"purge me, wash me, blot out my transgression."*

Sin deserves punishment – it is a legal or judicial matter. A standard has been violated, laws have been broken. Knowing his guilt, David asks for mercy. But sin also defiles the human heart, so you find David asking God for cleansing, for *inward washing* so he can praise and worship God. And sin disrupts relationship, so he pleads with God to *blot out* his transgressions and restore a right relationship. His guilty conscience is like dirty clothes, so he asks God to launder his conscience: *"wash me thoroughly."*

When you are really contrite before God, you don't pull up your track record of good deeds to kind of offset the weight of present guilt. You don't say to God, "I know what I did is bad, but I want to remind you of all the good things I've done."

Furthermore, a contrite person doesn't blame others for their part in his sin. David doesn't say anything in this prayer about Bathsheba! How guilty was she in all this? When you read about David seeing her bathing, sending a messenger to bring her to him, and of David's adultery with her, you don't find any evidence of Bathsheba saying no to David. As far as we know, she didn't refuse to come when the servant came to invite her to meet with the king. She didn't try to tell her husband what had happened when she had the opportunity. She seemed to cooperate in David's attempt to cover up her pregnancy.

I'm not blaming Bathsheba. In that time and place, she may have felt like she had no power to deny the king. I'm just pointing out that David doesn't blame her at all in his prayer. He's talking about his own sin, not hers. He makes it personal: *"I know, my sin, before me."* Since sin by definition implies a standard that has been violated – God's standard – all sin is ultimately against God, though it involves and impacts others. And only God can judge and forgive sin.

David's confession

We looked at the beginnings of David's confession in the last chapter. Let's consider the rest of it.

"Behold, I was brought forth in iniquity, and in sin did my mother conceive me. Behold, you delight in truth in the inward being, and you teach me wisdom in the secret heart" (Psalm 51:5-6).

David is not blaming his parents or saying there was something sinful about the way he was conceived. He's not saying his mother was a sinner. He's admitting his own moral powerlessness. He was born a sinner. From an early age, he was aware of right and wrong. But from the moment he was conceived, he has had a sinful heart.

Confession involves honesty before God. This is the truth: we are born with a sinful nature that leads us inevitably to sinful choices. God has built into all of us a basic sense of right and wrong. But we choose to violate our own consciences.

"Purge me with hyssop, and I shall be clean; wash me, and I shall be whiter than snow" (Psalm 51:7).

"Purge me with hyssop" is an allusion to Old Testament rituals of cleansing. A priest would dip a branch of the hyssop plant into water (or sometimes blood) and sprinkle the water on the people as a sign of cleansing. David's sin defiled him and made him unclean before God. He's asking both for forgiveness for the guilt of his sin and for cleansing from the stain of sin.

The rituals of atonement in the Old Testament foreshadowed the sacrifice Jesus would make on the cross. And the New Testament picks up the imagery of priestly cleansing from sin through sprinkling of blood:

"Therefore, brothers, since we have confidence to enter the holy places by the blood of Jesus, by the new and living way that he opened for us through the curtain, that is, through his flesh, and since we have a great priest over the house of God, let us draw near with a true heart in full assurance of faith, with

our hearts sprinkled clean from an evil conscience and our bodies washed with pure water" (Hebrews 10:19-22).

As an Old Testament believer, David didn't know how God would accomplish atonement through the substitutionary sacrifice of his own Son, but he is expressing his faith in God's atoning work: *"cleanse me like this, and I will be clean!"*

"Let me hear joy and gladness; let the bones that you have broken rejoice" (Psalm 51:8).

On the Day of Atonement, the high priest would lay his hands on a goat and confess the sins of Israel, symbolically transferring Israel's sins to that "scapegoat." The goat was then driven out into the wilderness, away from the camp of the people of Israel. In this visual symbolism, God taught his people that their sins would be laid on a substitute and carried away from God's presence. The priest then took a second goat's blood into the most holy place in the tabernacle and sprinkled blood on the mercy seat.

The people couldn't see the mercy seat, since only the High Priest was allowed to enter that room in the tabernacle (and later, the temple). But this symbolism taught them to understand how God saves. We deserve to die for our sin. Payment must be given to God for sin because God will not participate in any injustice. To overlook our sin as though we were not guilty would be unjust. But God accepts the death of a substitute in our place. When the priest sprinkled blood on the mercy seat, blood came between God and the sinner. On the basis of God accepting the blood of atonement, the priest could pronounce pardon. Those who looked in faith to God for forgiveness could know they were forgiven and accepted.

When you know you are guilty and deserve punishment for your sin and then hear God's pronouncement of pardon, the response is joy and gladness!

David is alluding to God's atoning work when he says, *"Let me hear joy and gladness; let the bones that you have broken rejoice."* He's saying, "Let me hear words of pardon and know that I will not be judicially crushed for my sin."

Restored relationship

"Hide your face from my sins, and blot out all my iniquities" (Psalm 51:9).

David's concern is not just to escape the punishment he deserved. He cared about what his sin had done to his relationship with God. He wants nothing to stand between himself and God. If God does not turn his face away from David's sins and put them behind him, David's sin will continue to mar his relationship with God.

If I say something to my wife that hurts her feelings, she doesn't suddenly stop being my wife. She doesn't stop loving me. But if I don't come to her and acknowledge the wrong I've done, it wounds our relationship. I can't feel close to my wife or expect her to feel close to me if I am unwilling to seek her forgiveness and be reconciled.

God doesn't stop being your Father when you sin. You don't lose your status as an adopted child of God. But you won't feel close to God when you hold on to sin. It will distance you from God. So David asks God to blot out his iniquities. Let there be nothing to mar his closeness to God.

Honest repentance is concerned about a restoration of an open and close relationship with God, not just about what other people might think of you if they know how you have sinned.

"Create in me a clean heart, O God, and renew a right spirit within me" (Psalm 51:10).

This is where repentance is different from just confessing your sin.

The prophet, Nathan, had told David that God forgave his sin and that he was not going to die, as he deserved, for his sins. But, just hearing an announcement of pardon is not enough to purge his deeply stained conscience. He needs inward spiritual grace from God, grace to believe God accepts him because the guilt of sin has been turned aside. He needs the grace to believe God has forgiven him. So he asks for inner transformation. He asks God to give him a changed heart and a right spirit.

People who confess their sins certainly feel a sense of relief. It feels good to not have to hide failure any longer. But a repentant person recognizes his weakness and inability to change. A repentant person knows his need for God to change his heart. David says, *"Create in me a clean heart..."* If you don't know that God cleanses you from the defilement of sin, that he washes away the dirtiness, you'll still feel dirty. You'll keep brooding on your failure, and your sin will define you. If your sin continues to define who you are, that is likely to produce repeated failures.

God is the Creator. We can't create a clean heart in ourselves, but God can. He can do what we are incapable of doing for ourselves.

"...and renew a right spirit within me." A right spirit means an internal attitude that is firm in purpose rather than a stubborn, rebellious spirit. He's not asking God to give him the gift of salvation (regeneration – a new heart). That God had regenerated his heart is evident in his repentant attitude! Instead, he's asking God to restore the kind of steadfast disposition he once had.

Intimacy with God

"Cast me not away from your presence, and take not your Holy Spirit from me" (Psalm 51:11).

In the ancient world, to be cast out of the king's presence meant being banished from the realm because you've displeased the king. For David to be cast away from God's presence would mean David's relationship with God was over. If God had cast him away from his presence, we wouldn't be talking about this psalm!

And what is God's presence? In one sense, every human being lives every moment of life in the presence of God. This is an inescapable reality. But for the people in the time of David, the presence of God was located in the tabernacle. In the Exodus story, when the tabernacle was completed, the glory of God came and settled over the tabernacle visibly. The glorious cloud that went before the people settled over the tabernacle. That meant God's presence was in the midst of his people. For David to be cast away from God's presence would mean being sent away from Jerusalem, away from the tabernacle, no longer welcome to come before God in worship.

When God showed David his sin, David's greatest concern was that he might lose the closeness of relationship with God that he longed for more than anything. That's the attitude of a repentant sinner – not just avoiding punishment, but a broken heart over what has been done to the relationship with God. There is an intimacy with God in this psalm that few other psalms can touch. Whatever temporal punishment would follow from his sin, he's asking God to keep him near the place where God's presence dwelt with his people.

"...and take not your Holy Spirit from me." The possibility of God removing the Holy Spirit from David did not mean taking away David's salvation. When David was anointed as King, God's Spirit set him apart to that calling and empowered him for that task. So David is asking that God not remove that empowering spirit that made him king.

To ask, "Do not take from me" implies that God had not done this. When King Saul sinned, God removed that anointing power from him. When Samson sinned, God took away his power. David is asking God not to do that in his case.

A willing spirit

"Restore to me the joy of your salvation, and uphold me with a willing spirit". (Psalm 51:12).

If David is going to keep on as king, with all the fallout that will result from this public sin, he needs a willing spirit, a kind of strength that comes from God to sustain joy in God's grace. He wanted a willing spirit – not being forced to suck it up and carry on as king – but a joy in the calling, a desire for it, and a willingness to serve God in that capacity.

What we need when we repent of our sin is a willing spirit to do what God says! We can't work up that kind of willing spirit by our own resolve and determination. We need God to give us that willing heart. Repentance involves an awareness of our own inability to do what we know God commands. All our resolutions and determination to do better will fall flat. We need God to continue to stir up a desire to obey him.

"Then I will teach transgressors your ways, and sinners will return to you. Deliver me from bloodguiltiness, O God, O God of my salvation, and my

tongue will sing aloud of your righteousness. O Lord, open my lips, and my mouth will declare your praise" (Psalm 51:13-15).

At first these words seem out of place in a prayer of confession and repentance. David is the big transgressor! But he's talking about teaching other transgressors about God's ways and helping sinners return to God. Why does he talk about teaching others God's ways?

A truly repentant person cares more about God's reputation than he does about his own. A repentant person is not self-absorbed and worried about what other people will think of him if they know about his sin. He's concerned about God's glory. Having been forgiven much, David had something to offer to other people who had fallen in sin and longed to be forgiven. If God could pardon David for adultery and murder, how much more would he forgive the sins of other people?

"For you will not delight in sacrifice, or I would give it; you will not be pleased with a burnt offering. The sacrifices of God are a broken spirit; a broken and contrite heart, O God, you will not despise" (Psalm 51:16-17).

We usually think of someone with a broken spirit as having lost all vitality and energy for living. To break a horse's spirit is to subdue him, to break his wildness so he can be ridden. David is saying his entire disposition has been humbled under God's mighty hand. A humble spirit is there in someone who knows he is helpless without God's grace. A person with a broken and contrite heart is the opposite of a self-made, hard-hearted person.

"Do good to Zion in your good pleasure; build up the walls of Jerusalem; then will you delight in right sacrifices, in burnt offerings and whole burnt offerings; then bulls will be offered on your altar" (Psalm 51:18-19).

Again, David's concern is for God's reputation and glory. If Jerusalem flourishes, its influence on the world increases, which brings greater glory to God. That's the desire of a person whose heart has been made tender to God by God's grace.

Finding mercy

When you hear people offer confession for some failure or sin, it often feels like it's all a self-centered show: I want to feel better. I want relief. I want my reputation restored. David was concerned more about God's glory. David knew his sin had provided an occasion for God's enemies to mock God and blaspheme. That broke his heart.

When you love someone selfishly, your focus is on what they can do for you. When you love someone well, your focus is on what is best for them! David's love for God is evident in his longing for God's name to be honored and glorified, despite the damage he had done to God's reputation.

When you are made aware of the depths of your sin, you know what it is like to stand before God in his terrifying holiness and feel ashamed and dirty. What you need most when you are aware of your sin is a Savior! You need to know that Jesus has bridged the gap that separates you as a sinner from God in his holiness. You need to know that he took the punishment your sin deserves and bore God's just wrath in your place that you might be washed, cleansed, sprinkled clean.

Jesus told a story about two men who went to the temple to pray. One told God about all the good things he had done and why he was worthy of God's love. The other could only say, *"God be merciful to me, the sinner."* Jesus said it is sinners who find mercy – those who are honest about what is in their hearts, honest about their guilt, transgressions and sin. It is sinners who come to God asking for mercy who find righteousness before God.

When you know you've been forgiven much, love for God grows stronger and praise for God becomes more joyful. Repentance is a gospel grace. It doesn't mean cowering in shame and guilt. It means running to God for grace and finding peace with God through our Lord Jesus Christ. The more God in his grace leads you to see your sin and repent of it, the greater your understanding of what Jesus has done for you will be, and that means wonder, joy, and gratitude will grow as you repent and believe the gospel over and over again!

May God make us repentant people!

PART VI

"Lead us not into temptation and deliver us from evil..."

EMPTATION is something all of us face in one way or another. We are tempted to do what God forbids or to choose some way of living that is not in keeping with God's commandments. Jesus reminds us to ask God to preserve us when we face temptation and to protect us from evil.

But what have you experienced when you asked God to remove a certain temptation from your life? Did that temptation just go away? God can certainly remove a particular temptation from your life, but often he doesn't. Why not? Why doesn't God remove the temptation, especially if it is in an area where you have struggled and failed often? You would think that removing the temptation from you so you no longer had to struggle would make growth in godliness easier. And doesn't God want you to grow in godliness?

What is hard to understand is that God might know better than you do what will bring the greatest growth in your life. If you didn't struggle with temptation, with disappointments, with questions about what God is up to, how would you learn to depend on him rather than depending on your own strength and determination? God knows what you need in order to learn dependence.

Psalm 62 encourages us to pour out our hearts to God and to rest in him alone rather than relying on human methods, determination or ingenuity. Can you trust God even when you can't understand what he is doing in your life? Times of testing of any kind are also opportunities for temptation, specifically, to reject what God says about his goodness and wisdom. Resting in God is not something that happens just by telling yourself to stop being anxious. Heart change is not something you work up by trying harder to do what is right. You can't change your restless heart by sheer willpower.

That's why dependent prayer is so important.

Chapter 12

God Alone

FEW YEARS AGO I had the opportunity to travel to Alaska for a couple of weeks to do some fishing and sightseeing. A long-time friend owns a fishing camp and invited me to spend a week with him at his lodge. As long as I was making the trip, I thought it would be fun to have my wife join me for a week after the fishing trip to see Denali National Park, Seward, and other tourist destinations.

I almost missed the connecting flight to the fishing lodge. My first plane flight was delayed a couple of hours leaving Orlando so I missed my connecting flight in Houston. I finally got to Seattle on the last flight out but, of course, missed my connecting flight to Anchorage. I arrived in Seattle at 2 a.m. and was placed on standby for a 5 a.m. flight, so I tried to catch a quick nap on the cozy Seattle airport floor. Every fifteen minutes, however, I was reminded to not leave my bags unattended.

I was able to get on that 5 a.m. flight, which landed in Anchorage just in time for me to catch the small plane that was graciously waiting to fly me out to my friend's lodge. If I had missed that flight, I would have had to arrange travel to the lodge on my own some two hundred miles west of Anchorage.

For three days, I enjoyed fishing with my friend and his guests at the isolated lodge on a beautiful Alaskan river. But the third night I experienced another sleepless night. About an hour after going to bed, I woke up in tremendous pain. It felt like someone was pushing a knife through my back. I thought maybe I had some kind of food poisoning, and managed to wait until morning to ask for help.

I was two hundred miles from the nearest hospital, in an area with no roads. My friend's son-in-law is a bush pilot, and he agreed to take me back to Anchorage in one of their little Cessna airplanes. We got close to Anchorage, but had to turn back because of a low cloud ceiling – those small planes have limits and no instruments for that kind of flying. He flew me to a nearby airport and I bought a ticket for a flight on a larger plane.

I finally got to Anchorage, rented a car at the airport and drove myself to the emergency room at the closest hospital, where the doctors confirmed my guess: I had a kidney stone. I was sent to a hotel to wait for it to pass.

It didn't pass!

My wife was scheduled to arrive in Anchorage for a week's travel, and I was somehow surviving from one pain pill to the next. When she arrived, we tried to drive to Denali National Park, to the Bed-and-Breakfast lodge where we had a reservation, but the pain of riding in the car was too much for me. We had to stop and find somewhere to stay.

A tiny stone was ruining the vacation I had looked forward to for many months and had planned so carefully. We finally had to go back to the hospital to have the stone removed surgically so I could get on an airplane to fly home.

I believe God is sovereign and that nothing that happens in my life happens by chance or without his control. Sometimes this belief causes frustration. God could have prevented all that trouble and pain, but he didn't. Was it really necessary for God to allow me to have a kidney stone then and there – on vacation? Why not a couple weeks later when I was back home? I had looked forward to that vacation for a long time. I had planned it out with great care. I had looked forward to enjoying Alaska with Margaret. Instead, I slept a lot (thanks to the pain medicine) and got out to see the sights only in short groggy spurts.

You've probably had weeks like that. You've probably had times when all you could think to pray was, "God, was this really necessary? What good purpose is there in these annoying things?"

You will speak hundreds, maybe thousands of words out loud today. But that's nothing compared to the flow of words in your mind and heart. In your mind there is a nonstop flow of words and thoughts: "God, why would you let this happen to me? Why do I experience so many disappointments and so much frustration? Why don't the plans that I make work out the way I hoped?"

What conversations are going on in your soul today? Are things noisy or quiet inside? When you turn off the television or the CD player or the computer; when you drive somewhere in silence with no music or talk radio; when you are really quiet, what words flow through your mind?

Abuse of power

Nobody is quite sure when Psalm 62 was written or what circumstances in David's life would fit this psalm. David was the king over Israel about 3,000 years ago, but we actually know a good bit about him.

He was the youngest son of a man named Jesse. Anointed to be king by the prophet Samuel during the reign of Saul, David endured a stormy relationship with Saul, who took to him like a son, and then turned around and tried repeatedly to kill him! David went into hiding, like an outlaw: he lived on the run with his growing band of men and, in the eyes of King Saul, they all became fugitives literally moving from cave to cave.

After many years of living on the run, Saul was killed in battle and David finally ascended to the throne. His reign is remembered as the golden era in Jewish history! Things went well for David until the episode with Bathsheba. David saw her bathing on a rooftop and used his kingly power to have her brought to his palace. When she told him she was pregnant, David again used his power to cover up his adulterous relationship and had her husband killed. Confronted by the prophet Nathan, David acknowledged his sin and came to real repentance.

God forgave his sin.

But trouble plagued his family the rest of his life! His last years saw an attempted coup by his son, Absalom, the rape of his daughter by another son, and the growing threat of division in his kingdom.

Peace amidst storms

Absalom's attempt to unseat David as king may be the background to Psalm 62. But to grasp the heart of this psalm, you don't need to know what moved the writer to pen these words. What he says here is what we all experience at different times in our lives. Just think of a time when you were restless. Think of a time when some unexpected problem rocked your life. Think of a time when it felt like everyone was against you.

Now consider this psalm and what it says about prayer.

"For God alone my soul waits in silence; from him comes my salvation. He only is my rock and my salvation, my fortress; I shall not be greatly shaken" (Psalm 62:1-2).

To wait in silence means to be quiet on the inside, to be at peace. Wouldn't it be nice to experience that kind of real internal peace, at least once in a while?

What David says in this little psalm is not a theoretical possibility. He says he had learned to live like this! This is not the kind of peace Buddhism teaches: "What you're experiencing is not real, it's an illusion." Buddhism tries to tell you pain is an illusion and you need to learn to meditate and empty your mind of all the fears and pains you're feeling.

At this point in David's life, waiting in silence before God did not mean he had no pressures or conflicts or problems, so everything was peaceful! His enemies were spreading lies about him (verse 4) and scheming to overthrow him. That's a pretty stressful situation!

The internal quietness he's describing is something he experienced in the midst of all kinds of stress, circumstances, and problems. And he didn't find peace by trying to empty his mind so he could pretend he didn't have any problems.

It was a learned composure. It wasn't just a feeling that came over him. It was something he had learned, something he had chosen. He chose to respond to life in a way that kept the internal words and images from taking control of his feelings and actions.

When we sing this psalm in our worship services, we say, "Find rest my soul in God alone." Literally, David said, *"For God alone my soul waits in silence."* Through all the ups and downs of his life, David knew God.

Consider what is described in I Samuel 30:

"While David and his men were away on a raid, the Amalekites raided their homes and carried off their wives and children as captives.

"David was greatly distressed because the men were talking of stoning him; each one was bitter in spirit because of his sons and daughters. But David found strength in the LORD his God."

The circumstances of that situation left David's men on the edge of despair. They were almost overwhelmed with distress and bitter feelings of disappointment. But David was able to find rest and strength in God. He had learned how to silence his mind and heart before God, even in painful, difficult circumstances.

Back to Psalm 62, verse 3:

"How long will all of you attack a man to batter him, like a leaning wall, a tottering fence?"

Recently, I went to YouTube to find the lyrics of a Christian song I wanted to hear. Below the lyrics was a dialogue of responses to the song. One man's response was full of vehement, ugly, hate-filled words against Christians. He claimed he didn't believe in God, so I was surprised he would go to the song in the first place. Why did he even bother to look at the words if he had such strong opinions against Christianity? But there it was – he felt compelled to write comment after comment against Christianity.

It could be that David is thinking of those who are opposing him, like the sad man spewing his hatred on YouTube toward Christians. He uses the analogy of their persistent attacks as being like a leaning wall or tottering fence that is about to fall down – either on themselves or on David. (Perhaps this is how David felt when his enemies taunted him as he was forced to run for his life from his own son, Absalom.)

Verse 4: *"They only plan to thrust him down from his high position. They take pleasure in falsehood. They bless with their mouths but inwardly they curse. Selah."*

Think about this

We usually skip over that word, *Selah,* like it's a Hebrew punctuation mark, a period at the end of a phrase. It actually is a word of instruction for the person singing this psalm. It means, "Stop and think about this. Take a long pause."

If David means his enemies are like a tottering fence that is about to collapse, he is saying they seem strong and firm, but their destruction is near. Ponder this truth! Those enemies who oppose you and who seem so strong and dangerous are really like a weak wall that is about to fall flat.

C.H. Spurgeon interpreted verse 3 as a description of what was about to happen to David's enemies, and our enemies: "they totter to their fall; it will be our wisdom to keep our distance, for no one is advantaged by being near a falling wall; if it does not crush with its weight, it may stifle with its dust."

David's enemies battered him, thinking they could throw him down and be done with him. If they could overthrow him with lies, they would delight in falsehoods! They might look like they're caring, concerned people just fighting for the truth, but their hearts were full of curses. But David knew how they would end up, because he knew the character of God.

"Selah." Pause and consider with amazement the futile violence of men who set themselves against God and his purposes. And remember the complete security that belongs to those who rest in God.

David continues, verse 5:

"For God alone, O my soul, wait in silence, for my hope is from him."

That sounds great, but how is it possible to rest (to be calm and silent inwardly) in those times when the world threatens to tear you apart? Only when you are convinced in your heart that God is with you can you wait for him and rest on him alone. Only when you are convinced he alone can meet your deepest need in the circumstances you are facing will you be able to rest in silence. When you feel like all you have, all you want, and all you expect are found in God, you can have joy, no matter what the circumstances of life.

Paul was in prison, facing death when he wrote:

"Rejoice in the Lord always. I will say it again, rejoice. Let your gentleness be evident to all. The Lord is near. Do not be anxious about anything, but in everything, by prayer and petition with thanksgiving, present your requests to God. And the peace of God, which transcends all understanding, will guard your hearts and your minds in Christ Jesus" (Philippians 4:4-7).

Out of control

In Psalm 131 David says he has stilled and quieted his heart before God. He says: *"I do not concern myself with great matters or things too wonderful for me"* (Psalm 131:1b).

That can't mean questions did not come into his mind. I'm sure he wondered what God was doing. It would have been natural for him to wonder why God was allowing difficult things to happen to him. When you experience troubling circumstances, you can't help but wonder why God tolerates evil things and why he doesn't make things better for good people and worse for people who don't honor him. Why doesn't God do what we think he should do?

David said he had learned an important truth: There are things he could not begin to understand *("I do not concern myself with great matters or things too wonderful for me")*. There are things I can't control. I have to leave those things in God's hands; they are beyond my ability to understand.

David had learned to make a choice: instead of dwelling on those things and being frustrated with what he didn't understand and could not control in the world around him, he had learned to leave those things in God's hands.

The result was a quiet mind and heart, a soul at rest in the Lord. David experienced a kind of quiet confidence.

Think of how much internal noise is stirred up in you. How much frustration do you experience because of anger about things you can't control? People don't do what you want them to do. Your children don't respond the way you think they should. Your husband doesn't say what you wish he would say. Your wife doesn't see the situation the same way you do. What if you could turn those things over to God and trust him with all your unanswered questions?

There are so many things you can't control, so many things you won't understand. Can you trust God with those things?

To trust God, you need to know why he is trust-worthy!

Refocus

When people face unexpected, serious difficulties, I often hear them say something like: "I just don't know if I can believe what I've been told about God. My faith is weak."

I don't think that's actually the problem. If you're trying to work up stronger faith, you're focus is on the wrong person. You're focusing on yourself and your ability to believe rather than focusing on God and his character.

Look at David's focus in Psalm 62:

"He only is my rock and my salvation, my fortress; I shall not be shaken.
On God rests my salvation and my glory; my mighty rock, my refuge is God"
(verses 6 & 7).

Notice how the psalmist makes this personal. Look back through the psalm and notice that he says, "*My* rock, *my* salvation, *my* fortress, *my* glory, *my* rock, *my* refuge!" It's not a general truth that God is all these things. It is the word "my" that makes all the difference. What good is it to know God is "a" refuge, "a" mighty rock if he isn't that for you personally? David lays claim to the character of God in action toward David!

He continues:

"Trust in him at all times, O people; pour out your heart before him; God is a refuge for us" (verse 8).

It's one thing to trust God when you can pretty well see what he is doing. It's another thing to trust him in those times when everything seems dark and you can't see what God is going to do.

But how do you know you can trust God?

Well, why do you think he told all these stories in the Bible of real people with real problems? They trusted God and found him to be their Rock, their Defender, their Fortress. To need a Rock, a Defender, a Fortress, a Refuge – to need saving implies that you are in trouble. It's when you are in a terrible storm and your boat is sinking that you need a refuge and a shelter from the storm. It is when you are surrounded by a hostile enemy that you need a strong fortress.

But, you might say, what about people who trust in God when they need a shelter and a fortress who are not delivered from their troubles? What about those people described in Hebrews 11 who had faith in God, but were killed? They died believing and trusting God. But notice they died! They weren't rescued at the last minute!

The writer of Hebrews said they died in faith, that is, they died believing God. What was it they believed about God? Was it just that he would rescue them from the immediate, physical danger or keep them from suffering? No!

Consider Shadrach, Meshach and Abednego before the King Nebuchadnezzar. When they were threatened with immediate, painful death in a blazing hot furnace for refusing to bow down and worship a statue of the king, they said, *"God is able to save us. But even if he doesn't, we won't bow down and worship the statue..."* (Daniel 3:17-18).

They were confident God had the power and ability to rescue them from the fire. But they were equally confident God could accomplish their ultimate deliverance from this fallen world by allowing them to die in the fire and taking them into his presence. Long before the Apostle Paul penned those beautiful words at the end of Romans 8, they believed that nothing in all creation could separate them from the love of God – not even death.

Selah

Again, Psalm 62 points us toward the trustworthiness of God:

"Trust in him at all times, O people; pour out your heart before him; God is a refuge for us" (verse 8).

What an amazing and beautiful admonition: *"pour out your heart before him."* Where else can you go with all this stuff in your heart? God's heart is opened to you in Scripture. Now you open your heart to him and tell him what you are thinking and feeling, what you're afraid of, what doesn't make sense to you. Don't hide anything from God (as if you could). Unburden your soul to him. Let him be the one you talk to about what you are thinking and feeling. Pour out your heart to God.

What a great invitation to honest, personal prayer. God is a refuge for you. He is a safe place. You can pour out your heart to other people, but they often can't handle what you tell them. You discover that people are quickly overwhelmed when you pour out your soul to them. But God is never overwhelmed. He can handle your questions and grief and disappointments.

At this point in Psalm 62, the writer again inserts the word, "Selah." Again, there's the need for a timely silence. Pause to think long and deeply about this.

He continues:

"Those of low estate are but a breath; those of high estate are a delusion; in the balances they go up, they are together lighter than a breath" (verse 9).

So often when we face difficult situations, we look for someone who can help us figure out what to do. We look for someone who can fix the problems for us. We look for human solutions to our problems.

Have you ever wondered why people can't help you figure out some of your difficult problems? The fact is people don't make very good gods! They can't be your defender the way God can! And the simple reason is they are *"but a breath."* They are mortal and finite.

But we keep trusting in human solutions. We think "if we can just get our political party in power, everything will change and all the wrongs will be righted." Certainly there is a place for political action, for working for what is best for society as a whole, and there is a time to fight for justice. But don't put all your hope in that. It's "but a breath" that leads to disappointment! Put your hope in God. Put your trust in him.

One word is enough

The Psalmist says:

"Put no trust in extortion; set no vain hopes on robbery; if riches increase, set not your heart upon them" (verse 10).

Spurgeon's comment on this verse is great: "Gain and fame are only so much foam on the sea. All the wealth and honor the whole world can afford would be too slender a thread to bear up the happiness of an immortal soul."

Don't set your heart on a solution money can provide. It's too unreliable! Psalm 62 concludes with these words:

"Once God has spoken; twice have I heard this: that power belongs to God, and that to you, O Lord, belongs steadfast love. For you will render to a man according to his work" (verses 11 and 12).

So unchanging and unchangeable is God, that we only need him to say something once! He is infallible: he doesn't make mistakes when he makes a promise. He is all powerful (omnipotent). One word of God's intentions is all it takes for God to do what he says.

But notice, *"twice have I heard this."* Maybe he means God said it, and he hears the echo of it in his soul again, and again. This is the message going around and around in the head of the psalmist: power belongs to God, and steadfast love. This is God's character. This is what God has revealed about himself.

David says, "This is what I will believe." God is able to do what he promises because power belongs to God. And God is willing to do what he promises, because he is a God of steadfast love. Therefore, trusting in God will not lead to disappointment.

"For you will render to a man according to his work" (Psalm 62:12b).

That's a difficult verse to interpret because we read it in terms of what we know about God's saving grace. We are justified by God's grace through faith in Jesus Christ, apart from any works that we bring to the table. David is not talking here about justification. He's talking about trusting God in difficult circumstances and resting in God's ability and goodness. It is more likely that what this phrase means in this context is that God will show himself powerful to those who trust him. Your trust in God (*"according to your work"*) will not prove empty. God will do what you are powerless to do.

For God to be your defender and fortress does not mean you will have no problems. We live in a fallen world. We are not spared the fallout of all that sin does to distort and disrupt life. God nowhere promises Christians that they will escape the pains and sorrows of life. What he promises is redemption. He will preserve you through whatever difficulties, problems and sorrows he chooses to allow in your life, and he will accomplish the final restoration of this world, the ultimate redemption (see the last half of Romans 8). Nothing will keep him from accomplishing what he has promised. Nothing will separate you from his love in Christ Jesus.

Instead of letting your desires, your fears, your opinions, your worries, or the things that irritate you take control of your life, you can choose to push them down and put them in their place.

How do you do that? Not by pretending your problems aren't real or that they aren't painful. Evil things that happen to you are still evil! Painful circumstances still hurt. It's not that you just empty your heart of all worries. Biblical faith is realistic. We do live in a broken, fallen, pain-filled world. But that brokenness is not the final word. It is not the ultimate reality. God's character is still one of steadfast love and his power has not diminished in the slightest. So don't let the difficulties and disappointments you experience rule your heart and mind.

Confidence in God

This is important to understand: you can't beat down the restlessness of your heart by sheer will power! You can try to tell yourself, "I will not be irritated by this. I will not let this bother me." But it won't work. Like the Scriptures ask, can the leopard change his spots? You can't do it! You're not strong enough! Your heart is too strong. And you can't change your heart just by telling yourself you need to calm down and think differently.

Biblical faith does not tell us "just don't let these things rule you." Instead, we are taught to replace the fears and restlessness in our hearts with something else. It's a process of replacing worries and the attitude that stirs up frustration in your soul with a confidence in God!

When your heart is filled with trust, it pushes out fear. When your heart is filled with confidence that God knows what is best for you and that what he has allowed is wise, you quit kicking against it. You rest in him when you trust him.

This is where prayer comes into the equation. When you know you can't change your own heart or overcome your fears and doubts by sheer willpower, turn to God in prayer and ask him to do in you what you are unable to do for yourself. Pour out your heart to him.

This is a huge part of the purpose of prayer. Page through the psalms and notice how often the psalmists pour out their confusion, their fears, their disappointments, and even their anger before God. They are not afraid to tell God what they are thinking and feeling! And as they do that, perspective returns!

You don't have to understand everything God is doing. You don't have to be able to explain what is happening in your life. You can trust God with those things if you are confident that he is for you, that power belongs to him, and that mercy and steadfast love are found in God.

"The secret things belong to the Lord our God, but the things revealed belong

to us and to our children forever, that we may follow all the words of this law" (Deuteronomy 29:29).

Will you believe that God is wise and that he is good? Will you trust that he is working in all things for the good of those he loves?

It is this kind of quiet confidence in God that develops as you learn to pour out your heart to him in prayer.

www.ingramcontent.com/pod-product-compliance
Lightning Source LLC
Chambersburg PA
CBHW051832090426
42736CB00011B/1774